Schöningh

EinFach
Englisch
Unterrichtsmodell

Series Editor: Hans Kröger

Robert Swindells

Daz 4 Zoe

by
Wiltrud Frenken
Angela Luz
Brigitte Prischtt

edited by
Hans Kröger

Vorwort

Einzelarbeit
Partnerarbeit
Gruppenarbeit
Unterrichtsgespräch
Schreibauftrag
Hausaufgabe
Audio-CD
filmische Präsentation
Projekt, offene Aufgabe
kreative Aufgabe
szenisches Spiel, Rollenspiel

Der Titel der Reihe **EinFach Englisch** verdeutlicht Zielsetzung und Programm zugleich. Einerseits soll Schülerinnen und Schülern auf einfache Art und Weise der Zugang zu klassischen, aber auch neuen literarischen Werken und Filmen ermöglicht werden, andererseits sollen Lehrerinnen und Lehrern in der Praxis erprobte Unterrichtsmodelle angeboten werden, die die wichtigsten methodisch-didaktischen Ansätze ihres Faches Englisch abdecken. Dabei sind die Modelle direkt, ohne langes Einlesen einsetzbar und stellen Unterrichtsarbeit konkret vor. Als besonders hilfreich für die Praxis haben sich dabei folgende Aspekte erwiesen, die für die Gestaltung der Reihe wesentlich sind:

- Überblick über **Figurenkonstellation**, ggf. **Filmszenen** und **Inhalt**
- **Klausuren** mit **Erwartungshorizont**
- **Arbeitsblätter**, **Tafelbilder** und **Leitfragen** für den Unterricht
- **Piktogramme** als Hinweise auf **Unterrichts-** und **Arbeitsformen**

Das Prinzip der „**Components**" ermöglicht darüber hinaus den variablen Einsatz der Modelle in unterschiedlich konzipierten Unterrichtsreihen. Dabei stehen Machbarkeit und Praxisnähe stets im Vordergrund.

**Das vorliegende Modell bezieht sich auf folgende Textausgabe:
Robert Swindells: *Daz 4 Zoe*, Cornelsen 2012, ISBN 978-3-06-033143-7.**

Sprachliche Betreuung: Anne Schülke

© 2013 Bildungshaus Schulbuchverlage
Westermann Schroedel Diesterweg Schöningh Winklers GmbH
Braunschweig, Paderborn, Darmstadt

www.schoeningh-schulbuch.de
Schöningh Verlag, Jühenplatz 1–3, 33098 Paderborn

Das Werk und seine Teile sind urheberrechtlich geschützt.
Jede Nutzung in anderen als den gesetzlich zugelassenen Fällen bedarf der vorherigen schriftlichen Einwilligung des Verlages.
Hinweis zu § 52a UrhG: Weder das Werk noch seine Teile dürfen ohne eine solche Einwilligung gescannt und in ein Netzwerk gestellt werden.
Das gilt auch für Intranets von Schulen und sonstigen Bildungseinrichtungen.

Auf verschiedenen Seiten dieses Buches befinden sich Verweise (Links) auf Internetadressen. Haftungshinweis: Trotz sorgfältiger inhaltlicher Kontrolle wird die Haftung für die Inhalte der externen Seiten ausgeschlossen. Für den Inhalt dieser externen Seiten sind ausschließlich deren Betreiber verantwortlich. Sollten Sie dabei auf kostenpflichtige, illegale oder anstößige Inhalte treffen, so bedauern wir dies ausdrücklich und bitten Sie, uns umgehend per E-Mail davon in Kenntnis zu setzen, damit beim Nachdruck der Verweis gelöscht wird.

Druck 5 4 3 2 1 / Jahr 2017 16 15 14 13
Die letzte Zahl bezeichnet das Jahr dieses Druckes.

Umschlaggestaltung: Jennifer Kirchhof
Druck und Bindung: Media-Print Informationstechnologie GmbH, Paderborn

ISBN 978-3-14-041170-7

Getting started

Have a close look at the picture and make a list of the topics it makes you think of.

Be prepared to explain your choice.

Robert Swindells: Daz 4 Zoe

The novel 6
The author 6
The content 7
The characters 7

Das Unterrichtsmodell 9
Vorüberlegungen zum Einsatz des Romans im Unterricht 9
Konzeption des Unterrichtsmodells 9
Weiterführende Materialien 11

Klausuren 12

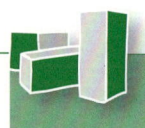

Component 1: Chippies vs Subbies 18

1.1 A world of contrasts 18
1.2 Love can change everything 26

Copy 1:   Analysing the style of language Daz uses 31
Copy 2:   While-reading assignments (pp. 8–12) 32
Copy 3:   Vocabulary log 34
Copy 4:   Black and white 35
Copy 5:   While-reading assignments (pp. 13–16) 36
Copy 6:   While-reading assignments (pp. 17–21) 37
Copy 7:   While-reading assignments (pp. 22–30) 38
Copy 8:   While-reading assignments (pp. 31–45) 39
Copy 9:   While-reading assignments (pp. 46–51) 40
Copy 10: Character and characterization in literature 41
Copy 11: Describing the behaviour of people 42
Copy 12: Character profile 44

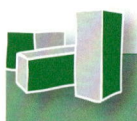

Component 2: Love in the time of suppression 45

2.1 First meeting 45
2.2 Domestic security 47
2.3 Choices 50

Component 2: Continued

Copy 13: While-reading assignments (pp. 52–64) **54**
Copy 14: While-reading assignments (pp. 65–83) **55**
Copy 15: While-reading assignments (pp. 84–97) **56**
Copy 16: While-reading assignments (pp. 98–104) **57**
Copy 17: File on Zoe **58**
Copy 18: Narrator and point of view **59**
Copy 19: Stylistic devices **60**

Component 3: A glimpse of hope in the desert 61

3.1 Flight into unknown territory **61**
3.2 Adventures in the unknown territory culminating in "High Noon" **67**

Copy 20: Comprehension (pp. 105–112) **75**
Copy 21: While-reading assignments (pp. 113–122) **76**
Copy 22: Dystopias: Definition and characteristics **77**
Copy 23: While-reading assignments (pp. 123–134) **78**
Copy 24: While-reading assignments (pp. 135–155) **79**
Copy 25: How to write a newspaper article **80**
Copy 26: Characterization grid **81**

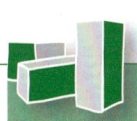

Component 4: What's left to say 82

Copy 27: Touch, turn, talk **85**
Copy 28: Blog **88**
Copy 29: Mediation: Abgeschlossene Luxus-Wohnsiedlungen, Reiche hinter Gittern **89**
Copy 30: Bob Marley and the Wailers: War **90**

The novel

The author

Robert Swindells is a bestselling English novelist for children and young adults. His books are so successful because they address challenging contemporary issues like homelessness, nuclear weapons, racial intolerance, bullying and religious extremism.

He was born in Bradford (Yorkshire, England) in 1939, the eldest of five children. He left school at the age of 15 (after failing his 11-plus exam) to become a copyholder. A few years later, in 1957, he joined the Royal Air Force for three years. After that he had many different jobs (shop assistant, advertising clerk printer and engineer). In 1967 he returned to school, taking evening classes and in 1969 he decided to train as a teacher. He discovered his interest in children's novels during his college years and wrote his first novel, *When Darkness Comes*, instead of writing an essay to complete his degree. It was published in 1973. He taught for eight years in Bradford before becoming a full-time writer in 1980.

Robert Swindells has earned critical acclaim and won prestigious awards for his writing, including the Children's Book Award for *Brother in the Land* in 1984, *Room 13* in 1989 and *Blitzed* in 2002; the Carnegie Medal for *Stone Cold* in 1994; the Sheffield Award for *Unbeliever* in 1996 and *Abomination* in 1999. His books have been translated into 21 languages, including Catalan and Innuit.

Selected works by Robert Swindells

When Darkness Comes (1973)
Dragons Live Forever (1978)
Brother in the Land (1984)
A Serpent's Tooth (1989)
Night School (1989)
Room 13 (1989)
Daz 4 Zoe (1990)
You Can't Say I'm Crazy (1992)
Stone Cold (1994)
Unbeliever (1995)
Smash! (1997)
Abomination (1998)
Invisible! (2000)
Blitzed (2002)
No Angels (2003)

The content

Robert Swindell's novel for young people, Daz 4 Zoe, is set in London in the not too far future. The reader meets Daz, a teenager who lives with his mother in a very run-down downtown area. In their apartment there is no electricity or running water. On the other hand, there is the other protagonist, Zoe, a teenage girl who lives with her parents in Silverdale, one of the privileged suburbs. The inhabitants of the downtown areas are called Chippies whereas the inhabitants of suburbia are called Subbies.

When Zoe accompanies some friends on an illegal trip to a club in the city, she accidentally meets Daz in the shady club Blue Moon and instantly falls in love with him. He cannot forget the pretty girl whom he saves from a dangerous situation in the club. Since he has helped out a group of Subbies his chances of joining Dred, a terrorist resistance group, are diminished. He had planned to join them and to take revenge for his brother who died fighting for Dred.

In order to meet Zoe again, Daz uses a secret tunnel system between the city, and the suburb. Fortunately, they can meet and they find out that they want to remain together no matter what obstacles there will be. Zoe's best friend, Tabby, has to leave Silverdale because her parents are found out to be members of FAIR, a forbidden Subbies' organization that fights for reconciliation between the two groups of inhabitants. A lieutenant Pohlman talks to Zoe because she is Tabby's friend and has stupidly written the word 'brainwashing' on a paper that she handed in at school. Her parents are very scared because of the visit of Domestic Security and decide to leave Silverdale, too, and to find a new home in a suburb that is 100 miles away from Silverdale.

Zoe decides not to leave Silverdale with her parents. She hides under a trash truck and leaves her home to stay with Daz and his mother. Meanwhile Daz has killed Peter, a member of Dred, because he overheard that he wanted to kill Tabby's family and rob them.

At the end of the novel there is a violent confrontation between the police and Dred in the course of which Zoe and Daz can flee.

The characters

Zoe May Askew Zoe is a 14-year-old student living in Silverdale, a very comfortable and pleasant suburb of London. She is an only child who does not have many friends. Her father is a real estate agent and so the family is quite well off. Zoe's life changes irrevocably when she meets Daz while being on an illegal trip to a shady club (Blue Moon) in the downtown area of London. She falls in love with him right away and even decides to leave her home and family in order to live with him in totally different surroundings.

Darren (Daz) Barren Daz is also a teenager (15) who lives with his mother in a very small apartment under very different circumstances from Zoe's comfortable life. His older brother has been killed while fighting for an illegal group of terrorists (Dred) against soldiers of the government. Daz dreams of joining that fight, but when he helps a group of young people from Silverdale to flee from a dangerous situation in the Blue Moon, he loses every chance of becoming a member of Dred. He is more than willing to forsake his dream as he has madly fallen in love with Zoe. When he uses a secret tunnel system, he makes enemies of violent members of Dred who fear that he will involuntarily give away this secret passage.

The novel

Zoe's grandmother	Zoe loves her grandmother very much and trusts her more than her parents. As becomes apparent later in the novel, her grandmother is a leading member of FAIR (Fraternal Alliance for Integration through Reunification) – an organization of inhabitants of the suburbs who think that society, as it is, is unjust and must be changed. She also was passionately in love with a young man when she was young – however, he did not take note of her. She can understand Zoe's feelings although she urgently warns her to give up her home and safe life there.
Daz's mother	Daz's mother – due to her awful living conditions - has aged prematurely and is depressed. She is marked by her poor surroundings. When Zoe flees – of all people – to her and her son she is shocked and realizes right away the terrible danger they are all in.
Tabitha Wentworth	The 14-year-old Tabitha, called Tabby, is Zoe's best friend. She invites Zoe to come Chippying with her and some friends, meaning that they go to a club in the city which is illegal. Since her father, a rich builder, is unmasked as a member of FAIR, the family is forced to leave Silverdale.
Pohlman	Lieutenant Pohlman is an officer of Domestic Security, the secret service of the government. His job is to find dissidents and to arrest them. His visit at the Askews' because of the friendship between Tabby and Zoe and a stupid remark Zoe made on a school paper, causes Zoe's parents to panic. They decide to leave Silverdale and move to another suburb far away.

Das Unterrichtsmodell

Vorüberlegungen zum Einsatz des Romans im Unterricht

Der 1990 erschienene Roman *Daz 4 Zoe* ist eines in der Reihe von Robert Swindells' Werken, die in einer dystopischen Gesellschaft angelegt sind und deren Protagonisten hauptsächlich junge Erwachsene darstellen, die gegen Ungerechtigkeiten oder Armut ankämpfen.

Der Autor lässt die beiden 15-jährigen Protagonisten Daz und Zoe in alternierend folgenden Abschnitten über ihre Situation und Liebe berichten. Sie stammen jeweils aus unterschiedlichen Vierteln ihrer Stadt: Zoe aus dem wohlhabenden, zum sogenannten *Subby-district* gehörenden Viertel Silverdale; Daz aus einem armseligen und verwahrlosten, im Zentrum gelegenen Viertel, welches zum *Chippy-district* gehört. Es gibt eine deutliche Zweiteilung in der geschilderten Gesellschaft, aufgrund welcher die *Chippy*-Bewohner dazu gezwungen sind, chancenlos und mittellos zu leben. Dennoch verlieben sich die beiden, was zur Flucht Zoes in das Viertel von Daz führt und schließlich nach aufregenden Ereignissen in ihrer gemeinsamen Flucht in ein neues Gebiet endet.

Der Roman eignet sich sowohl sprachlich als auch inhaltlich zur Einführung in die Romananalyse der Jahrgangsstufe 10 oder 11 und lässt sich in Unterrichtsreihen zu folgenden Themenbereichen einbinden: *dystopian societies, political systems, growing up, relationships and love in oppressive societies.*

In formaler Hinsicht lassen sich folgende Aspekte herausarbeiten: *point of view, characterization, language, register, tone, atmosphere, geographical telling names.*

Das Unterrichtsmodell ist so angelegt, dass die einzelnen Szenen sukzessive im Verlaufe der Besprechung des Romans gelesen werden. Die Lesearbeit wird motivierend durch die entsprechenden *Copies* mit *While-reading*-Aufgaben zum Inhalt sowie zur Wortschatzarbeit unterstützt.

Die Seitenangaben im Modell beziehen sich auf folgende Ausgabe:

Robert Swindells: *Daz 4 Zoe*, Cornelsen Verlag, Berlin 2012, ISBN 978-3-06-033143-7

Konzeption des Unterrichtsmodells

Das vorliegende Unterrichtsmodell thematisiert ausgewählte Aspekte des Romans, die in den einzelnen *Components* bearbeitet werden. Alle Seitenangaben beziehen sich auf die Textausgabe des Cornelsen-Verlages. Das Unterrichtsmodell ist so angelegt, dass der erste Abschnitt gemeinsam im Unterricht erarbeitet wird und die Kursteilnehmer dann im Laufe der Reihe sukzessive jeweils ein oder mehrere Abschnitte als Hausaufgabe lesen, begleitet von sehr unterschiedlichen Typen von *While-reading*-Aufgaben, die auf den *Copies* zu finden sind.

Component 1 bietet den Schülern über die Grafik der Einstiegsseite die Gelegenheit, sich den dargestellten Themen einer *segregated society* zu nähern und sich darüber auszutauschen. Daran schließt sich eine Phase der intensiven Beschäftigung mit der Sprache des Protagonisten an (*Copy 1*). Dies ist von grundlegender Bedeutung, um den Schülern das Verständnis der Lektüre zu erleichtern, da Daz in seiner Sprache stark vom *standard English* abweicht. Um den Wortschatz der Schüler lektürebegleitend zu erweitern, werden sie mit dem Führen eines individuellen *vocabulary log* (*Copy 3*) vertraut gemacht. Über eine erste Beschreibung und einen Vergleich der beiden Hauptfiguren wird der Begriff des *foil charac-*

ter eingeführt (*Copy 4*). Dann erfahren die Schüler im Verfahren des Expertenpuzzles, was *Subbies* und *Chippies* als Mitglieder der sehr unterschiedlichen Klassen voneinander halten. Der starke Kontrast zwischen den Gesellschaftsschichten wird auch durch die kreativ-produktiven Methoden des Visualisierens von Textinformationen zum *setting* und die schauspielerische Umsetzung einer Szene, in der beide Gruppen aufeinanderprallen, herausgearbeitet. Der inhaltliche Schwerpunkt des zweiten Teils von *Component 1* liegt auf den vom Autor angewandten Charakterisierungstechniken, die sich die Schüler anhand geeigneter Textstellen erschließen. Anschließend wird den Schülern ein Formular zum Erstellen eines *character profile* (*Copy 12*) vorgestellt, das sie im Verlauf der Lektüre für eine der Hauptpersonen ausfüllen.

In **Component 2** liegt der Schwerpunkt der Bearbeitung auf dem Training des Mündlichen. Sowohl in den *While-reading*-Aufgaben als auch in den Aktivitäten im Plenum werden die Schülerinnen und Schüler intensiv an Übungsformen des mündlichen Vortrags herangeführt. Sie müssen sowohl kleine Vorträge vorbereiten als auch in dialogischen Formen Arbeitsergebnisse präsentieren. Neben diesen Aufgaben werden grundlegende Aspekte der Romanbehandlung wie Erzählperspektive (*Copy 18*) und die Analyse von Stilmitteln (*Copy 19*) eingeführt und in Übungen vertieft. So soll ein Romanausschnitt in eine andere Erzählperspektive gesetzt werden oder ein Auszug auf Stilmittel untersucht werden. Als kreative Aufgabe wird auf Basis des Verhörs, das Pohlmann mit Zoe durchführt, eine Akte über Zoe angelegt (*Copy 17*).

Component 3 bezieht sich auf die Seiten 105 bis 155. Die Aufgabe der Charakterisierung von Daz, Zoe und Grandma, die sich durch den gesamten *Component* durchzieht, besteht im Ausfüllen des *characterization grid* (*Copy 26*), der seitenweise weitergeführt wird. Am Ende von **Component 1** wird mit *Copy 12* eine Vorlage für ein *character profile* angegeben, welches im Laufe der Besprechung des Romans mit Informationen zu Daz, Zoe oder Grandma ausgefüllt wird. Am Ende von *Component 3* werden sowohl zum *characterization grid* als auch zum *character profile* in Bezug auf Zoe, Daz und Grandma mögliche Lösungen vorgestellt. Jeweils am Anfang einer Stunde bzw. als Hausaufgabe wird eine *While-reading*-Aufgabe zu den in Blöcken zusammengefassten Seiten gestellt. (*Copy 20, Copy 21, Copy 23* und *Copy 24*). Der *Component* beginnt mit einer *chessboard activity* als Gruppenarbeit, in welcher verschiedene, für die gezeigte dystopische Gesellschaft wichtige Vorschläge und Themen aufgelistet sind, die von verschiedenen Seiten her beleuchtet und bewertet werden können.
Um die Auseinandersetzung mit dem Text auch auf der gesprochenen Ebene anzuregen, werden die Schülerinnen und Schüler aufgefordert, sich gegenseitig Abschnitte des Romans laut und intoniert vorzulesen. Diese Übung wird schon im ersten *Component* dargestellt, ist sie doch von umso größerer Bedeutung, als Daz sich in einer schwer verständlichen *slang*-Sprache artikuliert. Auch hier sollen die von Daz verfassten Teile in ein verständliches Englisch umgewandelt werden.
Ein weiterer methodischer Aspekt liegt auf kreativen Aufgaben wie dem Verfassen eines *newspaper article* und der Darstellung der Gefühle und Gedanken von Zoes Mutter, nachdem sie von Zoes Flucht erfahren hat. Das Verfassen eines *newspaper article* wird durch Hinweise zur Vorgehensweise auf *Copy 25* vorbereitet.
Ein weiteres Augenmerk liegt auf der Auseinandersetzung mit dem Roman als Beispiel eines dystopischen Romans. Im methodischen Ansatz von *expert groups* werden die auf *Copy 22* dargestellten Merkmale einer dystopischen Gesellschaft hinsichtlich ihres Auftretens im Roman untersucht.

In *Component 4* werden verschiedene Übungsformen und Textsorten angeboten, mit deren Hilfe man sowohl den Inhalt rekapitulieren kann (*Touch, turn, talk*) als auch vertiefend auf einzelne Aspekte des Romans eingehen kann. Dabei ist *Copy 28* mit Blogeinträgen britischer Teenager, die das Buch gelesen haben und sich in ganz unterschiedlicher Weise dazu äußern, ein Ausgangspunkt für das Verfassen einer eigenen Kritik. *Copy 29* bietet den Ausschnitt aus einem deutschen Artikel zum Thema *gated communities* und regt dazu an, sich mit dem Thema zu beschäftigen.

Auf *Copy 30* findet sich ein Songtext von Bob Marley, der Menschenrechte auch für unterprivilegierte Menschen fordert.

Weiterführende Materialien

Robert Swindells:
http://www.penguin.co.uk/nf/Author/AuthorPage/0,,1000050055,00.html

Literaturdidaktik:
- Collie, Joanne/Slater, Stephen: *Literature in the Language Classroom*. Cambridge University Press 1987
- Nünning, Ansgar/Surkamp, Carola: *Englische Literatur unterrichten*. Grundlagen und Methoden. Stuttgart: Klett 2006

Onlineartikel und Internetseiten:
- http://news.bbc.co.uk/2/hi/uk_news/6984707.stm (*"Class segregation 'on the rise'"*)
- http://www.independent.co.uk/news/education/education-news/school-intake-segreated-by-class-7618824.html (*"School Intake 'segregated by class'"*)
- http://www.telegraph.co.uk/education/universityeducation/8313880/Nick-Clegg-attacked-by-Tories-over-university-admissions.html
- http://www.guardian.co.uk/world/2009/jan/06/brazil-rio-slum-barrier (*"Rio Slum Barrier Plans Spark Outcry"*)
- http://articles.latimes.com/2003/dec/19/opinion/oe-low19 (*"Imprisoned by the Walls Built to Keep 'the Others' Out"*)

Filme:
- *La Zona. Betreten verboten.* Rodrigo Plá
- *London-Capital under strain.* Documentary. Carole Greco, Camille Robert. Frankreich 2012
- *Auf der sicheren Seite.* Dokumentation Lukas Schmid, Corinna Wichmann. Deutschland 2010
- *In Time.* Andrew Nicoll. USA 2011

Romane:
- Blackman, Malorie: *Noughts & Crosses*. London: Corgi Books, 2002
- Collins, Suzanne: *The Hunger Games Trilogy, 3 Volumes*, English Scholastic, UK, 2008 – 2011

Songs:
- Bob Marley and the Wailers: *War*. Album: *Rastaman Vibrations*. Island Records 1976
- Michael Jackson: *They don't care about us*. Album: *HIStory. Past, Present and Future, Book I*. Epic 1996

Klausuren

Klausur 1 ist ein Auszug aus dem letzten Teil des Romans *Daz 4 Zoe*. Bevor man sie stellen kann, muss **Component 2** bearbeitet worden sein, da es in der Aufgabenstellung um die in diesem *Component* behandelten Themen *stylistic devices* und *point of view* geht. Die Schülerinnen und Schüler müssen den Roman zu Ende gelesen haben, da sie in Aufgabe 1 die Textstelle in den Zusammenhang des Romans einordnen sollen.

Die Klausur hat 599 Wörter und ist sprachlich einfach, da sich die Schülerinnen und Schüler an den Stil des Romans gewöhnt haben werden.

In **Klausur 2** sollen die Schüler einen Zeitungsartikel bearbeiten, in dem eine Rede des britischen Erziehungsministers Michael Gove wiedergegeben wird, in der er anhand des Themas Schule herausstellt, dass Großbritannien immer noch eine undurchlässige Klassengesellschaft ist. Die Klassenzugehörigkeit der Eltern (und nicht etwa die Begabung) ist der ausschlaggebende Faktor für die berufliche Zukunft eines Kindes. Können die Eltern eine teure Privatschule nicht bezahlen, hat das Kind keine Chance auf eine gute Stelle. Er betont, dass die einflussreichen Posten zum allergrößten Teil in den Händen der Absolventen der Privatschulen sind, obwohl diese nur 7 % der Bevölkerung darstellen. Michael Gove bezeichnet diesen Zustand als moralisch unhaltbar.

Mit 630 Wörtern ist die Klausur sowohl für einen Grund- als auch für einen Leistungskurs geeignet. Der inhaltliche Bezug des Textes zu *Daz 4 Zoe* besteht in der auch im Roman (in gesteigerter Form) beschriebenen Gesellschaftsordnung, in der die Reichen die Welt regieren und die Armen nicht teilhaben lassen wollen. Formal sollten die Schüler mit der Analyse von Sachtexten (speziell auch politischen Reden) vertraut sein.

Robert Swindells: Daz 4 Zoe (pp. 153–154)

The shot, and the agonised scream which followed it echoed deafeningly through the basement. Sick with horror, yet driven by a compulsion I was powerless to resist I turned. Daz, supported by Mick and Smithy, was still on his feet. Cal was kneeling on the floor with his arms wrapped round his stomach, screaming. His broken glasses lay
5 in a crimson splotch on the floor. As I gaped, the two men let go of Daz and turned towards the stairs. I turned, too. Pohlman was crouching on the bottom step with a smoking gun in his fist. Smithy was raising his own weapon when Pohlman fired again. The gunman spun round and crumpled, his pistol skittering away across the cement. Mick, seeing Pohlman momentarily distracted, doused his torch and made a
10 dash for it, knocking the policeman sideways and leaping on to the stairs. There was a shot, a cry and a metallic clatter. A light which had been shining from somewhere behind Pohlman went out and the basement was plunged into blackness.

A grip clamped my arm, Daz yelled, "Come on!" and I was dragged, totally blind, across the floor. I don't know how he knew where to go, but almost at once I tripped on the
15 first step and then we were climbing. There was a heck of a racket – shouting, shooting, some sort of motor. Anyway, there we were, going up into blackness and then I saw light – a glimmer and some flashes and we were up in the lobby and somebody had a spotlight on it so I couldn't see much more in the dark.

I'm not sure, but I think we were shot at as we burst out on the street. Who shot at us
20 I don't know – it might've been Dred, or the cops, or both. Or they might've been shooting each other and we got in the way. Anyway, Dred was there in strength to engage the cops in a fire-fight, and that's what saved us. We ran through the flash and rattle of small arms fire and everybody was too busy keeping their heads down to worry about us. DS had a fan on the roof of the block and as we set off along the street
25 it came swooping down, chasing us with its spot lamp, but when it slowed to keep pace with us it became a soft target for Dred, whose concentrated fire forced it to climb away. We ran on, gasping and sobbing, and when we stopped there was darkness all around and the light was far behind.

We rested briefly to catch our breath and to marvel at our escape. I told Daz about the
30 letter and what had happened at school. Daz hugged me and said I was a hero and I said no, he and his mother were the brave ones, and then suddenly we both burst into tears, which never happens to heroes in the movies.

We weren't safe yet, of course, and so once we'd got our breath back and dried our eyes and decided which way was west we moved on quickly, intent on putting as much
35 distance as possible between ourselves and the city by dawn.

I was hungry, which isn't surprising when you remember I hadn't eaten anything all day unless you're going to count Grandma's letter, but I was too happy to care. We'd almost died, but here we were alive. Instead of the end we were moving toward the beginning of something. I knew we were. I felt it getting closer.
40 I could feel it getting closer.

Approximately 599 words (page 153) from DAZ 4 ZOE by Robert Swindells (Puffin, 1990) © Robert Swindells, 1990. Reproduced by permission of Penguin Books Ltd.

compulsion strong desire to do s.th.

crimson dark red
splotch large mark or spot
to gape to stare with your mouth open
to skitter to move very quickly

in strength in large numbers

to marvel to be very surprised

Assignments

1. Describe which events lead to the action depicted in this excerpt of the novel. Explain the names mentioned.

2. Analyse the author's use of language in creating an atmosphere of tension in this excerpt. Take into consideration point of view and stylistic devices.

3. a) Discuss the question if *Daz 4 Zoe* presents a possible future of our society.
   or: b) Imagine Zoe and Tabby meet a couple of years after the events described in the novel. Write a dialogue.

Erwartungshorizont zu Klausur 1

Zu 1: Zoe has been forced to leave the school where she had been hidden by Mr James because the police search the premises. Daz is hunted by Dred because Cal has worked out that he has killed his friend, Pete – he hides in the basement of his apartment block. When Zoe shows up at Daz's home she is caught by Dred and used to force Daz to come out of his hiding place. When Cal starts torturing Daz the police appear.

Cal is the leader of the terrorist group called Dred. Mick and Smithy are Cal's friends and accomplices. Pohlman is a lieutenant at Domestic Security (DS), an agency that controls the inhabitants of Silverdale and Rawhampton.

Grandma is Zoe's grandma, the most important member of FAIR, a secret Subby group that fights for reconciliation between Chippies and Subbies. The letter that Zoe has eaten gave her instructions on how to get to the new home of the Wentworths.

Zu 2: This excerpt is told by a first-person narrator, Zoe. ("I" – l. 2) She also addresses the reader directly when she says "when you remember …" (l. 36). She describes the events in the basement in an almost breathless way (short sentences) which attributes to the atmosphere of tension in this passage.

The author uses a number of stylistic devices that contribute to this atmosphere, e.g.

tricolon	There was a shot, a cry … (ll. 10/11) shouting, shooting, … (l. 15)	These tricola underline the hectic atmosphere of the situation and the fact that things are very chaotic.
antithesis	sick with horror – driven by a compulsion (l. 2) almost died – were alive (l. 38) the end – the beginning (ll. 38 f.)	These antitheses show that the situation is very dangerous and that the outcome is not decided.
parallelism	said I was – I said no, he and his mother were. (ll. 30 f.)	It shows that both are impressed with the courage each one has proven.
joke	I hadn't eaten all day unless … (ll. 36 f.)	This joke shows how relieved Zoe is that they are still alive.
metaphor	basement was plunged into darkness (ll. 12)	This metaphor underlines the dark and dangerous situation.

Zu 3: a) Students should point out that there are tendencies in our society to separate different classes (schools, parts of cities, jobs…). There is a general feeling of a society divided into a small group of very rich and influential people and a big group of disadvantaged and poor people who have to struggle to make a living. On the other hand, however, there are no agencies like Domestic Security in our government and it is hard to imagine that we would erect borders between inner cities and suburbs as described in the novel.

Zu 3: b) Students' answers will vary; however, they should point out in which way the girls' lives have developed. Has Tabby found a new safe home? Is her father still active for FAIR? Has Zoe found true love with Daz? Has, maybe, the system finally collapsed?

There should not only be private information but also some explanation of how society has moved on.

Michael Gove:
Public school domination 'morally indefensible'

Jessica Shepard, Education correspondent
The Guardian, Thursday 10 May, 2012

Education secretary blames failure of politicians to tackle public school stranglehold on positions of power in the UK.

The dominance of the public schoolboy in every prominent role in British society is "morally indefensible", according to the education secretary.

Michael Gove said the sheer scale of privately educated men in positions of power in business, politics, media, comedy, sport and music was proof of a "deep problem in our country".

Politicians have failed to tackle the issue with "anything like the radicalism required", he admitted in a speech to independent school headteachers in Brighton. In England, more so than almost any other country, the privileged are likely to stay privileged and the poor are likely to stay poor, he said.

"Around the cabinet table, a majority, including myself, were privately educated," Gove said. He added that the shadow chancellor, shadow business secretary, shadow Olympics secretary, among others, were also educated at private schools.

"On the bench of our supreme court, in the precincts of the bar, in our medical schools and university science faculties, at the helm of FTSE 100 companies and in the boardrooms of our banks, independent schools are – how can I best put this – handsomely represented," he said.

Just 7% of the English population are educated privately, but half the UK's gold medallists at the last Olympics went to independent schools, Gove said. Quoting *Luck*, a book by Ed Smith, a former England cricket player turned journalist, Gove said Britons were 20 times more likely to play for England if they had attended a private school. While 25 years ago, only one of the 13 players representing England on a cricket tour of Pakistan went to a fee-paying school, that figure had risen to two-thirds. "The composition of the England rugby union team reveals the same trend," Gove said.

The stars of British comedy, theatre and TV were predominantly from public schools, he said, citing Hugh Laurie, David Baddiel and Armando Iannucci. "Popular music is populated by public schoolboys," he said, giving Chris Martin of *Coldplay* and Tom Chaplin of *Keane* as examples.

But the public school "stranglehold" was strongest in the British media, Gove argued. The chairman of the BBC and its director-general, as well as many national newspaper editors, were former private schoolboys, he said.

"Indeed, the Guardian has been edited by privately educated men for the last 60 years. But then, many of our most prominent contemporary radical and activist writers are also privately educated," he said. "George Monbiot of the Guardian was at Stowe, Seumas Milne of the Guardian was at Winchester and perhaps the most radical new voice of all – Laurie Penny of the Independent – was educated here at Brighton College.

"I record these achievements not because I wish to either decry the individuals concerned or criticise the schools they attended, far from it … It is undeniable that the individuals I have named are hugely talented and the schools they attended are premier league institutions, but the sheer scale, the breadth and the depth of private school dominance of our society points to a deep problem in our country.

"More than almost any developed nation, ours is a country in which your parentage dictates your progress," he said. "Those who are born poor are more likely to

stay poor and those who inherit privilege are more likely to pass on privilege in
50 England than in any comparable country. For those of us who believe in social justice, this stratification and segregation are morally indefensible."
Britain was "squandering our greatest asset, our children" because they were not achieving their potential. The coalition's education reforms were helping more schools prove "destination need not be destiny", Gove said.

to squander: to carelessly waste money, time, opportunities etc.

(630 words)

Copyright Guardian News & Media Ltd 2012.

Assignments

1. Point out why Michael Gove, the British education secretary, states that public school dominance in positions of power is 'morally indefensible' (l. 4).

2. Examine the means he uses to make his attitude convincing to his listeners/readers.

3. You have a choice here:

   a) Comment on Michael Gove's statement that "More than almost any developed nation, ours is a country in which your parentage dictates your progress," ... (ll. 46f.).

   or

   b) Put yourself in the position of a parent from the underprivileged class who cannot afford to send his intelligent child to a public school. Write a letter to the editor voicing your opinion about Gove's statements on social segregation.

Erwartungshorizont zu Klausur 2

Zu 1: Michael Gove, the British education secretary, states that the positions of power in British society are clearly in the hands of those who graduated from a public school. He thinks this situation reveals a social injustice. The families who can afford to pay the fees of a public school are only very few (7% of the population). Yet they represent the vast majority in the important positions in business, politics, comedy, sports, music and in the media. Thus, a member of the underprivileged class has no chance to achieve a higher position. A child born into a poor family will remain poor whereas a child born into a wealthy family will remain wealthy. Michael Gove blames the politicians for this social segregation and lack of social mobility. He accuses them of wasting the potential of so many intelligent children who cannot achieve their best because their parents are too poor to send them to a public school.

Zu 2: Michael Gove employs various means to convince his audience of his opinion that this situation of social injustice is wrong. For example:
- metaphor: stranglehold (ll. 1 f.)
- enumerations (l. 6, ll. 13 f., ll. 15 – 17)
- examples (ll. 13 f., ll. 28 – 30, ll. 36 – 38)
- numbers, statistics (ll. 19 – 26)
- quote (ll. 20 ff.)
- reference to famous, popular people (ll. 27 – 30)
- euphemism (l. 18)

Zu 3: a) Answers will vary here. However, it is to be expected that students will discuss the question whether the British class system is morally acceptable. They will probably defend the idea of social justice and point out some measures as to how the government could promote social mobility to give everybody the chance to fully use his /her potential. They may refer to the situation of extreme social segregation described in the novel *Daz 4 Zoe* as a possible development in a dystopian future.

b) Again, answers will vary, but the formal aspects of how to write a letter to the editor must be fulfilled. The content of the letter should clearly express the opinion of an angry parent who blames the politicians for being unable to give his/her child the chance to achieve his full potential and improve his life. Students may describe the situation and frustration of the parent and suggest some measures on how the government could improve the situation for future generations.

Component 1
Chippies vs Subbies

Als Einstieg in die Arbeit mit Robert Swindells Jugendroman *Daz 4 Zoe* bietet die Grafik der Einstiegsseite (über Folie, Beamer oder vergrößert als Poster präsentiert) den Schülern die Möglichkeit eines persönlichen Zugangs zu den dargestellten Themen, die die Problematik einer „unmöglichen Liebe", der Diskriminierung, der Segregation, der sozialen Unterschiede, Ungerechtigkeit sowie der Praktiken eines totalitären Staates sowie der Rebellion aufgreift. So kommen die Schüler miteinander ins Gespräch und bringen ihr Vorwissen ein. Am Ende der Reihe (oder auch in deren Verlauf) kann man auf die Grafik zurückkommen und konkret auf die im Roman zur Sprache gekommenen Aspekte hin interpretieren.

Im *Placemat*-Verfahren gehen die Schüler in Vierergruppen so vor, dass sie sich zunächst allein über die dargestellten Themen Gedanken machen und diese jeder in seine Ecke des *placemats* einträgt. Dann wird das Blatt im Uhrzeigersinn gedreht und sie lesen die Einträge der anderen. Anschließend diskutieren sie ihre Ideen und einigen sich auf vier Themen, die als die wichtigsten in der Mitte des Blattes als gemeinsames Ergebnis festgehalten werden. Abschließend präsentieren alle Gruppen, die Vorschläge werden an der Tafel festgehalten und anschließend kategorisiert, sodass sich folgendes Tafelbild ergeben könnte.

> Make a list of the topics the picture makes you think of.
> Categorize the topics.

situation	state policies	people's reactions	personal aspects
• the gap between rich and poor • social injustice • social segregation • discrimination • inequality • different worlds • class differences • separate lives • …	• suppression • oppression • surveillance • "Big Brother" • a watchful society • a totalitarian system of government • dictatorship • …	• crossing barriers • rebellion • disrespecting the rules • questioning the laws • …	• the power of love • strict parents • …

1.1 A world of contrasts

Der Beginn der Lektüre des Romans soll im Unterricht durch gemeinsames Lesen der ersten Seiten erfolgen. Daz, der 15-jährige Protagonist, stellt sich in den ersten zehn Zeilen vor. Er ist ein ungebildeter *Chippy*, der in der völlig heruntergekommenen Innenstadt *Rawhampton* mit seiner depressiven Mutter lebt und sich mit dem Gedanken trägt, der illegalen *Dred*-Organisation beizutreten, um seinen Bruder zu rächen, der von der Polizei erschossen wurde. Er benutzt einen sehr informellen Stil der gesprochenen Sprache mit vielen Unkorrektheiten und rein phonetischer Schreibweise. Diese Sprache wird den Schülern bei der ersten Begegnung befremdlich, vielleicht sogar unverständlich sein, aber nach einer Klärung der wichtigsten Abweichungen vom *standard English* werden sie sich schnell daran gewöhnen. Aus diesem Grund soll der Romanbeginn (S.7) sehr kleinschrittig im *Think-pair-share*-Verfahren zunächst rein sprachlich in folgenden Schritten bearbeitet werden: lautes Vorlesen,

Verbessern der Orthografie, Umschreiben in *standard English*. Anschließend werden die Abweichungen systematisch erfasst.

Copy 1: Die Schüler erhalten zunächst in einer Phase der Einzelarbeit die Gelegenheit, sich dem Text individuell zu nähern, indem sie sich über die Aussprache und Intonation der Wörter und Sätze klar werden. (Ein Wörterbuch sollte zur Verfügung stehen). Dann lesen sie den Text einem Partner vor und klären eventuelle Unsicherheiten bezüglich der Aussprache. In Partnerarbeit schreiben sie den Text nun in orthografisch korrektem Englisch auf und vergleichen ihre Ergebnisse mit einem weiteren Paar. Dann wird der Text wiederum in Partnerarbeit in *standard English* umgeschrieben und im Plenum präsentiert. Der letzte Schritt besteht darin, übergeordnete Begriffe für die unterschiedlichen Kategorien zu finden, in die die sprachlichen Abweichungen von der Standardsprache einzuordnen sind. Zur Binnendifferenzierung können für schwächere Schüler die Kategorien vorgegeben werden und die Schüler finden ein passendes Beispiel aus dem Text.

In einem kurzen Unterrichtsgespräch wird schließlich ausgehend von der Frage "What does it tell us about Daz?" die Funktion besprochen, die Daz' Sprachstil zukommt.

Lösungsvorschlag zu *Copy 1:*

1. Correct spelling
   Daz they call me. Two years back when I come thirteen Del, that's my brother, they catch him raiding with the Dred. Top him, don't they, and I'm just gone fifteen.
   Two law and orders come tell our mum, one woman, one man, no, they don't come till after they done it never. Our mum been down a long time then with the dulleye, and she just sort of stares don't she, till they go off, and it's not till night she cries.
   She says don't you never go off with no Dred, our Daz.
   No mum, I says, but I never crossed my heart. Don't count less you crossed your heart, right?

5. Standard English
   They call me Daz. Two years ago, when I turned 13, they catch /caught Del – that's my brother – raiding with Dred. They kill /killed him, don't / didn't they, and I've / had just turned 15.
   Two police officers, a woman and a man, come/ came to tell our mother, and they don't come till after that, either. Our mother has/ had already been down with a depression for a long time and she just sort of stares/stared doesn't/ didn't she, until they leave /left. And she only starts /started crying in the night.
   She tells /told me never to join Dred.
   No mum, I say /said, but I didn't cross my heart. It doesn't count unless you cross your heart, right?

7. Daz's style of language

feature	quotation
incorrect spelling	"wen" (l. 1), "gon" (l. 3), "crost" (l. 9)
numbers written in figures	"2 years" (l. 1)

feature	quotation
phonetic spelling	"brovver" (l. 1), "wiv" (l. 2), "wumin" (l. 4)
contracted forms	"don't you" (l. 8)
question tags	"don't thay" (l. 2)
rejoinders	"rite?" (l. 10)
parenthesis	"Del that's my brovver" (l. 1)
elision	"dunnit" (l. 5)
informal/colloquial words/expressions	"top" (l. 2), "dulleye" (l. 6)
short words	"call, years" (l. 1)
absence of sophisticated vocabulary	
simple sentences	"Daz thay call me." (l. 1)
incomplete sentences	"Top im don't thay" (l. 2)
incorrect grammar	"I sez" (l. 9), "Don't count" (l. 9)

➡ The author uses the language to characterize Daz as a poorly educated person. His social background is probably very poor.

Zur Vertiefung des inhaltlichen Verständnisses notieren die Schüler in der Hausaufgabe fünf Fragen, die die ersten Zeilen des Romans aufwerfen. Außerdem lesen sie die Seiten 8–12 und bearbeiten die entsprechenden *while-reading assignments* auf **Copy 2**. An dieser Stelle wird den Schülern auch das *vocabulary log* (**Copy 3**) vorgestellt. Als *ongoing homework* trägt jeder Schüler hier pro Abschnitt des Romans 1–2 Wörter seiner Wahl ein. Er verpflichtet sich, diese Wörter zu lernen und aktiv anzuwenden.

Zu Beginn der nächsten Stunde (wie auch in allen folgenden Stunden) stellen ein paar Schüler die Wörter vor, die sie für ihr *vocabulary log* ausgewählt haben. Danach tragen sie im Plenum die Fragen vor, die an der Tafel festgehalten werden. Anschließend besprechen sie in Kleingruppen von drei Schülern die *while-reading assignments*.

Questions that arise while reading the opening section of the novel (p. 7)

- What/who is Dred?
- Why/where did Del raid?
- Who killed him?
- Why did they kill him?
- Why does the mother suffer from depression?
- What does his mother's depression mean for Daz?
- Why doesn't Daz honestly promise not to join Dred?
- What about his father?
- …

Lösungsvorschlag zu *Copy 2. a) while reading pp. 8 –11:*

1. Zoe's dad is an estate agent, he sells houses. (p. 8, ll. 19 f.)
2. Her life is boring and her age is lousy. (p. 8, l. 28)
3. Because they live in the suburbs. (p. 9, ll. 6 f.)
4. To protect themselves from the robberies of the Chippies. (p. 9, ll. 16 f.)
5. Chips are their favourite food. (p. 9, l. 27)
6. They feel bored and imprisoned. (p. 10, ll. 1 –10)
7. Cigarettes, alcohol, drugs and cool music. (p.10, ll. 14 f.)
8. The Chippies want their money and they hate them. (p. 10, ll. 23 – 26)

Lösungsvorschlag zu *Copy 2. b) while reading p. 12:*

1.

Daz's style	Standard English
graft	work
veezaville	suburb
peanuts	money
doodys	clothes
to top	to kill

2. He refers to the Falkland Wars, a 1982 armed conflict between Great Britain and Argentine over the Falkland Islands (South Pacific) which was won by the British.

3. Mr James explains that the Falklands Wars made some people rich and the British society became divided into different classes.

4. Daz's mother doesn't want him to join Dred. Daz feels he has no other choice but to become a member of Dred. They kill Subbies. You have to be 15 to join them.

Component 1: Chippies vs Subbies

Nun sollen die beiden Protagonisten näher betrachtet und miteinander verglichen werden. Dazu finden die Schüler in arbeitsteiliger Gruppenarbeit Adjektive, die ihren ersten Eindruck von Daz bzw. Zoe beschreiben, und notieren gleichzeitig ein passendes Antonym. Bei der Besprechung der Ergebnisse wird sich so bei den meisten Adjektiven wohl ergeben, dass das jeweilige Antonym auf die jeweils andere Figur zutrifft und die Schüler den angelegten Kontrast erkennen.

Group 1: Having read page 7, what is your first impression of Daz? Find six adjectives that describe him. Then write down their antonyms. Use a dictionary if necessary.

Group 2: Having read page 8, l. 1 – p. 9, l. 13, what is your first impression of Zoe? Find six adjectives that describe her. Then write down their antonyms. Use a dictionary if necessary.

Ein mögliches Ergebnis könnte folgendermaßen auf Folie festgehalten werden.

adjective	antonym
poor	rich, wealthy
impolite	polite
unfriendly	friendly
taciturn	talkative
poorly educated	highly educated
serious	funny, humorous
brief	descriptive
inarticulate	articulate
worried	bored, carefree
unhappy, angry	happy
caring	
…	…
Daz	**Zoe**

➡ contrast, difference, opposite

Zur Verdeutlichung der vom Autor geschaffenen Kontrastfiguren und deren Funktion sowie zur Einführung des literarischen Fachbegriffs *foil* erhalten die Schüler **Copy 4**, auf der ein kontrastreiches Bild und eine Definition abgedruckt sind.

Lösungsvorschlag zu *Copy 4*:

1. The picture, as well as the characters, represent stark contrasts. Black and white are opposing colours, the circle and the triangle are contrasting shapes, the dots and the lines are different patterns. The creation of the foil characters can be seen as analogous because they are characterized by very different, opposing traits.

2. Daz and Zoe are introduced as very different characters. They can be described by opposing adjectives. Daz's poverty seems to emphasize Zoe's wealth (and vice versa), and Daz's seriousness becomes more obvious when compared to Zoe's humour.

Das Thema der krassen Unterschiede vertiefend soll nun untersucht werden, was Daz und Zoe als Repräsentanten ihrer jeweiligen sozialen Schicht voneinander halten. Hierbei zeigen sich vorurteilsbedingte Antipathien auf beiden Seiten. Zoe gibt die radikale Meinung ihres

Vaters wieder, äußert aber auch Zweifel an deren Gültigkeit. Daz hat sich aufgrund seiner bitteren Erfahrungen eine eigene Meinung gebildet und einen Groll gegenüber den Subbies entwickelt. In einer Art Expertenpuzzle suchen die Schüler zunächst in arbeitsgleichen 4er-Gruppen Zoes Aussagen über die Chippies, Zoes Aussagen über die Subbies, Daz' Aussagen über die Chippies oder Daz' Aussagen über die Subbies heraus und und schreiben jede Aussage auf einen Papierstreifen. Im nächsten Schritt bilden sie neue 4er-Gruppen, sodass je ein Schüler aus den vorigen Gruppen in jeder Gruppe vertreten ist. Dabei ist es hilfreich, jede der vier Gruppen mit farblich unterschiedlichen Papierstreifen auszustatten, damit die Bildung der Gruppen einfach und schnell zu überprüfen ist. Jetzt stellen sie sich ihre Ergebnisse vor und legen die Papierstreifen so zusammen, dass die Aussagen (wenn möglich) in Beziehung zueinander erscheinen. Dann werden die Ergebnisse über den OHP präsentiert.

Step 1: Get together in groups of four.

Group 1: Reread p. 9, l. 4 – p. 10, l. 26 and make a list of the statements Zoe makes about Chippies.

Group 2: Reread p. 9, l. 4 – p. 10, l. 26 and make a list of the statements Zoe makes about Subbies.

Group 3: Reread p. 12 and make a list of the statements Daz makes about Chippies.

Group 4: Reread p. 12 and make a list of the statements Daz makes about Subbies.

Step 2: Get together in new groups of four, consisting of one member of each former group and present your findings. Compare Daz's and Zoe's statements and arrange them in an appropriate way.

Step 3: Present your findings to the class and explain.

What Zoe and Daz say about Chippies

Zoe	Daz
• Call them Subbies • Don't work • Hang out • Live in crummy apartments • Don't wash • Hate Subbies • Envy Subbies • Want their cars and nice houses, but don't want to study or work • Get so many handouts (don't need to work) • Steal • Watch Subbies all the time • Know how to have a good time • Have exciting night clubs with drugs and cool music • Don't have money • Kill Subbies • Are dangerous	• Would work, but there are no jobs • Can't wash because they often don't have water • Are dirty and funny
➜ prejudice negative ideas	➜ explanation, no contradiction, no disagreement

Component 1: Chippies vs Subbies

What Zoe and Daz say about Subbies

Zoe	Daz
• Are called Subbies because they live in the suburbs • Work ⟶ • Take showers ⟶ • Have nice houses ⟶ • Ordinary, decent people • Do what people ought to do • Need fences and guards to protect themselves from the Chippies ⟶ • Call them Chippies because their favourite food is chips • Go out to meet Chippies because it is exciting ⟶ • Kids get bored • Feel imprisoned • Kids do have money to spend ➡ positive ideas, but also doubts	• • Talk about Chippies • They've got work • They've got water • They've got money • They've got big cars and new clothes • Are well off with their fences and guards • … • … • Come out to Chippy nightclubs • "I hate Subbies" • Before the Falklands War there were no Subbies and no Chippies (no classes) • The world would be better without Subbies ➡ resentful confirmations attempt to find an explanation for the social divison

Hausaufgabe ist die Lektüre der Seiten 13 – 21 und die *While-reading*-Aufgaben/*Copies 5* und *6*.

Diese Aufaben werden am Ende der folgenden Stunde im Plenum oder in Kleingruppen besprochen. Zuvor soll die Raumdarstellung in den Fokus dieser Stunde rücken. Die extremen Unterschiede zwischen den im Roman entworfenen sozialen Klassen werden in den Figuren sowohl als Individuen als auch als Zugehörige ihrer Klasse und auch in der Beschreibung ihres Umfeldes deutlich. Deshalb sollen auch die Raumdarstellungen der reichen Vorstadt *Silverdale* und der armen Innenstadt *Rawhampton* miteinander verglichen werden. Zunächst werden die Informationen über *Silverdale* in arbeitsgleichen Kleingruppen aufgelistet und Adjektive gesucht, die den Eindruck wiedergeben und die Atmosphäre erfassen.

> In small groups, re-read pp. 8 – 12 and make a list of the information the reader gets on Silverdale. Then find four adjectives that describe your impression of the setting and three adjectives for the atmosphere that is created.
>
> **Silverdale**
>
> - a suburb in England (p. 8, l. 6)
> - beautiful architect-designed houses (p. 8, ll. 13 f.)
> - rich residents (p. 8, l. 13); nice houses (p. 9, l. 7); cars (p. 9, l. 12)
> - fences and guards to protect them
> - squash clubs, health clubs, bridge clubs, youth clubs (p. 10, l. 11 f.)
> - water (p. 12, l. 9)
> - fast cars (p. 12, l. 10)
> - fences, dazzlers and bouncers (p. 12, l. 11)
>
> ➡ wealthy, rich, posh, elegant, high-class, … but also fenced-in, separated, …
>
> **atmosphere:** calm, safe, serene, carefree (but also fearful), friendly, inviting, positive, easy, optimistic, …

Der Schwerpunkt liegt jedoch auf der Untersuchung der Innenstadt. Um sich in den Ort des Geschehens hineinzuversetzen, setzen die Schüler die Beschreibung in ein Bild um und stellen es einem Partner vor, mit dessen Bild sie ihres vergleichen und diskutieren.

Visualizing Rawhampton

1. Read Zoe's description of *Rawhampton* (p. 17, l. 6 – p. 18, l. 8).
2. Close your eyes and try to see the place in your mind.
3. Draw a sketch of what you imagine it to be like. (Your drawing does not have to be a perfect piece of art!)
4. Show your picture to your partner and explain what you saw in your mind.
5. Talk about what is the same or different in your pictures.
6. Read the text again to prove your point or to find possible new ideas.
7. Agree on four adjectives that describe your impression of *Rawhampton* and three for the atmosphere that is created.

Rawhampton

- Derelict houses, some burned out
- Cracks in the road with weeds poking through
- Piles of brick and glass and cement everywhere
- The street lights are not working
- Piles of trash along the road
- Deep holes in the road, filled with slimy water
- Thin, lonely dogs (some big)
- Multi-storey apartment blocks scattred across a wilderness of longgrass and overgrown pathways
- Doorless and glassless buildings
- Rubbish everywhere: cans, bottles, plastic bags, mattresses, baby-buggies

➡ poor, dilapidated, wild, derelict, ruined, appalling, squalid, unhealthy, dangerous, …

atmosphere: depressing, frightening, desolate, tense, alarming, nightmarish, eerie, gloomy, hostile, joyless, …

Lösungen zu *Copy 5*:

pp. 13 – 16:

1. wrong: p. 13, l. 5: Friday night; 2. right: p. 14, l. 9; 3. right: p. 14, ll. 20 – 25; 4. wrong: p. 15, l. 18: "the smile cut no ice". p. 16

1. a, c; 2. a; 3. b

Lösungsvorschlag zu *Copy 6*:

correct order: 4 – 8 – 1 – 6 – 9 – 3 – 7 – 2 – 5

Hausaufgabe zur nächsten Stunde ist die Lektüre der Seiten 22 – 30, begleitet von den *While-reading*-Aufgaben auf *Copy 7*.

Component 1: Chippies vs Subbies

1.2 Love can change everything

Auf den Seiten 22 – 51 beschreiben die beiden Protagonisten (jeweils aus ihrer Sicht), wie sie sich im *Blue Moon* kennen gelernt haben und nicht mehr vergessen können. Beide sind sich bewusst, dass ein Wiedersehen oder gar eine Beziehung gegen alle Regeln der Gesellschaft und des Staates verstoßen und ihr Leben total verändern würde. Trotz aller Zweifel an den Gefühlen des anderen und trotz der zu erwartenden Probleme sind sie bereit, Risiken einzugehen und denken darüber nach, wie sie sich wieder treffen könnten. Dabei kommen die Konsequenzen schon zum Tragen, bevor sie sich überhaupt wiedertreffen. Zoe lehnt sich gegen die politischen Überzeugungen ihres Vaters auf, verärgert ihre Freunde und bekommt auch in der Schule Probleme wegen Tagträumereien und Aufmüpfigkeit. Daz hat seine Chance auf eine Mitgliedschaft bei Dred verspielt, seine Freunde gegen sich aufgebracht und muss die Schule ohne Abschluss verlassen. In dieser Situation treten die Persönlichkeitsmerkmale der beiden Hauptfiguren deutlich zu Tage. Außerdem lernt der Leser in diesem Teil des Romans Zoes Großmutter kennen und erfährt mehr über ihren Vater.

Zu Beginn der Stunde tauschen die Schüler sich über den Inhalt anhand der Besprechung der Hausaufgabe (*Copy 7*) aus.

> **Lösungsvorschlag zu *Copy 7*:**
>
> 1. Because she is different.
>
> 2. a) p. 23, l. 3   b) p. 23, ll. 7–11   c) p. 23, ll. 20 – 26
>   d) p. 24, l. 3   e) p. 24, l. 13   f) p. 24, ll. 20 f.
>
> 3. Daz came to the *Blue Moon* to become a member of Dred, an organization that kills Subbies because they hate them. But when he sees Zoe he likes her immediately, despite the fact that she is a Subby girl.
>
> 4. Larry (a Subby boy) tries to flirt with a Chippy girl and insults the Chippies. They get angry and attack him. Daz takes care of the dangerous situation by leading the Subbies out of the club safely.
>
> 5. a) "I can't believe it. You're one of us, for Christ's sake! Why didn't you fight on our side? You want to be a member of Dred? You're a traitor, that's what you are".

Dann soll das Verhalten der Jugendlichen beim Aufeinanderprallen der gegensätzlichen Bevölkerungsgruppen in der Bar näher betrachtet werden. Da es sich um eine spannende Szene handelt, die ohne viel Aufwand im Klassenraum gespielt werden kann, bietet es sich an, diesen Textabschnitt (pp. 27– 28) schauspielerisch umzusetzen. Zur Vorbereitung werden nonverbale Kommunikationsmittel in einer kurzen unterrichtsvorbereitenden Phase gesammelt und an der Tafel notiert.

Which non-verbal means of communication do you know?

---

non-verbal means of communication

visual
- facial expression
- gestures
- movement

acoustic
- intonation
- pitch
- volume of speech
- speed of speech

Component 1: Chippies vs Subbies

Die Szene erfordert einen Regisseur, elf Schauspieler und einige Statisten. So könnten die meisten Kurse wohl in zwei Gruppen mit folgender Aufgabenstellung arbeiten:

Act out the scene

Your task is to act out the scene where the Subbies get into trouble with the Chippies in the Blue Moon. (pp. 27 – 28)

- Think about the props you'll need.
- Choose a role:

Subbies	Chippies
Zoe	Daz
Tabby	pretty girl
Larry	her boyfriend
Ned	her girlfriend
	boyfriend
	beefy guy 1
	beefy guy 2
	further guests of the bar

- Nominate a director.
- Discuss how to present the scene. Think of gestures, facial expression and intonation.
- Rehearse your interpretation.
- Perform the scene for your classmates.

Nach der Präsentation und deren Evaluation wird die Hausaufgabe gestellt: die Lektüre der Seiten 31 – 51, unterstützt durch die *While-reading*-Aufgaben auf den **Copies 8** und **9**.

Zur Sicherung des Textverständnisses beginnt die nächste Stunde mit der Besprechung der Hausaufgaben in Partnerarbeit, in Kleingruppen oder im Plenum.

Lösungsvorschlag zu *Copy 8*:

1. a) to mope (p. 33, l. 1): Zoe feels sad, sorry for herself because she wants to meet Daz again, but thinks it is almost impossible.

   b) even (p. 31, l. 12): Zoe uses this word to emphasize that she knows that nobody of her friends would expect a Chippy to be a hero.

   c) puzzled look (p. 31, l. 24): Zoe's behaviour is so unusual that her mother is confused; she does not understand what is happening.

   d) gorgeous (p. 34, l. 30): Zoe uses this word to express that she thinks Daz is extremely handsome or attractive.

   e) to neglect sth. (p. 35, l. 12): Zoe's grandma was so absorbed by her thoughts about the boy that she did not pay any attention to the things she had to do at work.

   f) to be in a fix (p. 32, l. 21): Zoe finds herself with a problem that is difficult to solve because Subbies and Chippies do not socialize.

   g) to stick your neck out for sb. (p. 31, ll. 5 f.): Since Daz helped the Subbies to get out of the dangerous situation, thus being disloyal to his class, he risked being attacked or rejected by the Chippies.

h) to be out of the question (p. 33, l. 21): Zoe is sure that her parents would say that seeing Daz is definitely not possible or not allowed.

2. Daz feels ambiguous about having met Zoe. On the one hand, he has fallen in love with her and can't stop thinking about her. On the other hand, he wishes he hadn't met her because, by helping the Subbies, he missed his chance of becoming a member of Dred. Moreover, he thinks that Zoe is a Subby who despises Chipppies, but still she has kissed him. He is very confused and knows that he cannot talk to his teacher about his problem and that his mother would not appreciate a relationship with a Subby girl.

3. a) … she does not see a chance to leave Silverdale and meet Daz.

   b) … brutally shoot at the Chippies to stop the riot.

   c) 1. She does not know how to meet Daz. 2. She has arguments with her dad. 3. Her friends feel neglected and turn away from her. 4. She has trouble at school because she thinks of Daz and does not pay attention to her class.

4. Daz is a Chippy and has always been convinced that Dred is good and Subbies are bad. Now that he has fallen in love with a Subby girl, he is not so sure any more. So he repeats his old opinion mantra-like to get out of this confusion.

5. The Dennison government deprived the Chippies of their right to vote by introducing the Franchise Income Qualification in 2004. But Miss Moncrieff gives another reason and makes Zoe write this lie forty-five times.

Lösungsvorschlag zu *Copy 9*:

1. a) Clint was supposed to do a job for Dred together with Del. But, the night before, Clint was drunk and he gave out information to the wrong persons.

   b) He showed him a tunnel that leads from Rawhampton to Silverdale.

   c) He will get shot.

   d) There are many tunnels and you can get lost easily.

   e) Daz wants to use the tunnel to get to Zoe.

2. 1) wrong   2) right   3) wrong   4) wrong

3. Daz wants to use the tunnel to get to Silverdale. Then he will look for a school for secondary education and wait at the end of the day to see Zoe when she leaves school.

Diese Textabschnitte eignen sich auch zu einer systematischen Annäherung an den Themenkomplex *character and characterization*. Dabei verschaffen die Schülerinnen und Schüler sich zunächst einen allgemeinen Überblick über die Möglichkeiten eines Autors, eine Figur zu charakterisieren (*showing and telling technique*). Ausgehend von den über Folie oder Tafel präsentierten einfachen, eindeutigen Beispielen gelangen die Schüler in einem Unterrichtsgespräch zu der Erkenntnis, dass ein fiktionaler Charakter direkt oder indirekt vom Autor gezeichnet werden kann. Als Ergebnis kann sich folgendes Folien- bzw. Tafelbild ergeben.

Component 1: Chippies vs Subbies

• Describe the differences between these two ways of characterizing a person.

Zoe about herself: "I'm not the kind of kid who gets in trouble at school, I don't get mad at teachers, I get scared." (p. 48, ll. 24f.)	Zoe about herself: "Anyway, I sat looking at it, and then I pulled the last sheet towards me and scrawled 'Brainwashing' across the bottom." (p. 44, ll. 14f.)
Zoe about the Chippies: "Chippies're envious, see. Full of hate." (p. 32, l. 17)	Zoe about the Chippies: "You let a Chippy stay the night, he'll rip off all your stuff and maybe cut your throat for an encore." (p. 32, ll. 15f.)
→ direct (explicit) characterization telling technique	→ indirect (implicit) characterization showing technique
The author (the narrator) informs the reader directly about the characteristic traits of a person by using adjectives.	The reader has to infer what a character is like by interpreting his behaviour or thoughts and words.

Zur Vertiefung und zur Verdeutlichung, dass ein Autor innerhalb eines Werkes mit beiden Techniken arbeiten kann, wie im obigen Beispiel schon gezeigt, werden die Schüler nun aufgefordert, in Partnerarbeit ein Beispiel für jede der Techniken auf den Seiten 33 – 36 zu finden, auf denen Zoes Großmutter vorgestellt wird.

• Find an example on pp. 33 – 36 where Zoe uses the telling technique and an example where she uses the showing technique to let the reader know what her grandma is like. Work with a partner.

Zum Beispiel könnten folgende Stellen des Romans genannt werden:

Telling technique:

- "She's got all her marbles." (p. 33, ll. 6f.)
- "She sees things differently." (p. 33, l. 9)
- "Grandma has a quick mind but her legs are slowing down some." (p. 34, l. 3)
- "She's terrific, old Grandma." (p. 34, ll. 9f.)
- "Grandma's not like that. She takes the time to listen." (p. 34, l. 13)

Showing technique:

- "She smiled when she opened the door." (p. 34, l. 4)
- "She put me in a chair and fixed coffee like she was the kid and I was the old lady." (p. 34, ll. 15f.)
- "I'm saying it's a possibility you should bear in mind, Zoe. It could save you some pain, though of course it'll cause you some, too." She smiled. (p. 35, ll. 24f.)
- "[…] she stroked my hair. Neither of us spoke for a while, and then Grandma said, still stroking my hair […]" (p. 36, ll. 5f.)

Component 1: Chippies vs Subbies

Im Anschluss daran können in einem Unterrichtsgespräch (unter Rückgriff auf den zu Beginn behandelten Aspekt der Sprache) die Aspekte herausgestellt werden, die für eine Charakterisierung wesentlich sind. Die Ergebnisse werden in Form eines *clusters* an der Tafel festgehalten, brauchen aber nicht von den Schülerinnen und Schülern abgeschrieben zu werden, da sie auf der Kopiervorlage *Characterization* (**Copy 10**) abgedruckt sind. Hierauf stützt sich auch das *characterization grid*, das in **Component 3** Anwendung findet.

Which aspects can give us information about a person's character?

Dann sollen die Schüler das Verhalten von Zoe und Daz im ersten Teil des Romans (pp. 7 – 51) näher untersuchen, indem sie in Partnerarbeit die Aufgaben auf **Copy 11** bearbeiten. Anschließend werden die (sicher unterschiedlichen) Ergebnisse im Plenum diskutiert.

Lösungsvorschlag zu *Copy 11*:

adjective	noun	adjective	noun
impolite	impoliteness	insecure	insecurity
understanding	understanding	disrespectful	disrespect
indifferent	indifference	selfish	selfishness
rebellious	rebellion	irresponsible	irresponsibility
supportive	support	excited	excitement
sympathetic	sympathy	cool	coolness
self-confident	self-confidence	protective	protection
helpless	helplessness	caring	care
hostile	hostility	mature	maturity
courageous	courage	proud	pride
anxious	anxiety	envious	envy

Hausaufgabe zur nächsten Stunde ist das vorläufige Ausfüllen des *character profile* (**Copy 12**) für Daz, Zoe oder Grandma mit den Informationen, die der erste Teil des Romans (pp. 7 – 51) liefert. Der Lehrer erklärt, dass diese *character profiles* weitergeführt werden und im Laufe der Lektüre durch relevante neue Informationen ergänzt werden. Außerdem werden die Seiten 52 – 62 gelesen, unterstützt durch die *while-reading assignments* auf **Copy 13**.

Analysing the style of the language Daz uses

1. Read the text (p. 7, ll. 7–10) to yourself. Focus on pronunciation and intonation. If necessary, use a dictionary. Be prepared to read the text to your partner.

2. Find a partner and read out the text. Then listen to your partner read the text.

3. Together with your partner, rewrite the text using correct spelling.

4. With your partner, find another pair of partners and compare your texts.

5. Together with your partner, transform the text into *standard English*. Consider grammar as well as vocabulary.

6. Present your version to the class, discuss and agree on the best solution.

7. Looking back at the changes you made, find categories to give a general description of the features that characterize Daz's style of language. Write down the term and give an example

While-reading assignments (pp. 8–12)

a) While reading pp. 8–11, answer the following questions. Indicate the page(s) and line(s) where you found the answer.

1. What does Zoe's dad do for a living?

2. What does Zoe say about her life and her age?

3. Why do the Chippies call Zoe and her family and friends Subbies?

4. Why do the Subbies have fences and guards?

5. Where did the Chippies get their name from?

6. Why do the Subbies go chippying?

7. What can you find in a Chippy club?

8. Why is it dangerous for Subbies to go to Chippyville?

b) **While reading p. 12:**

1. Find four words that are characteristic of the language Daz uses. Write them down with the corresponding standard English expressions.

Daz's style	Standard English

2. Find out what Daz means by "Britain won the fork lands" (l. 12)

3. How does Mr. James explain the existence of Chippies and Subbies?

4. What does the reader get to know about Dred?

Vocabulary log

While reading *Daz 4 Zoe* choose one or two words from each section and add them to the list. Learn these words and use them as often as possible.

word, page, line found	definition	collocation/example	translation (German word)
to raid (p. 7, l. 2)	1. (police): to make a surprise visit to search for something illegal	Police found weapons when they raided his home.	eine Razzia durchführen
	2. to go into a place and steal things	The gang raided three homes in the area.	einbrechen, plündern

Black and white

1. Look at the picture and explain the link to the comparison of Daz and Zoe.

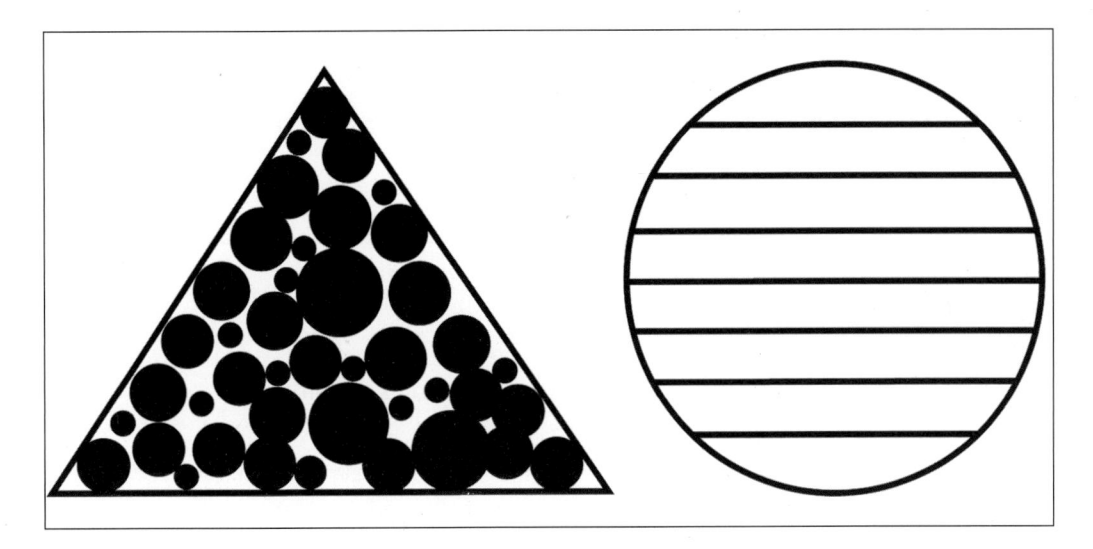

2. Read the following definition of the literary term *foil* and give reasons why Daz and Zoe can be described as foil characters.

> **foil**: in literature, a character who is presented as a contrast to a second character so as to point to or show to advantage some aspect of the second character. An obvious example is the character of Dr. Watson in Sir Arthur Conan Doyle's Sherlock Holmes stories. Watson is a perfect foil for Holmes because his relative obtuseness makes Holmes's deductions seem more brilliant.
>
> Reprinted with permission from *Encyclopædia Britannica*, © 2013 by Encyclopædia Britannica, Inc.

While-reading assignments (pp. 13–16)

1. pp. 13–15

Right or wrong?

	right	wrong
1. Tabby asks Zoe to go chippying on Saturday night.		
2. Zoe is very nervous because she will have to lie to her parents.		
3. Zoe thinks Tabby has only invited her because she needs Zoe's cousin as an alibi.		
4. The bouncer is impressed by Ned's open smile.		

2. p. 16

Tick off the correct statements.

1. Mick
   - ☐ a) is Daz's friend.
   - ☐ b) asks Daz fo fight for him.
   - ☐ c) is a member of Dred.

2. Daz
   - ☐ a) wants to leave school and become a member of Dred.
   - ☐ b) plans to take the Veeza-Teeza test to go to a Subby school.
   - ☐ c) is ready to do what his mother says.

3. The *Blue Moon*
   - ☐ a) has got a swimming pool.
   - ☐ b) is the place where Daz wants to meet Cal.
   - ☐ c) is a night club for adults.

While-reading assignments (pp. 17–21)

Put the sentences of this summary into their correct order so that they tell the story as it happens.

1. While driving in the car, Tabby, Larry and Ned tell Zoe what the Chippy clubs are like.

2. Zoe sees a very attractive boy.

3. The bouncer explains that Chippies don't have any money.

4. Zoe and her friends drive through the derelict streets of the outskirts of Rawhampton, then pass a desolate residential development on their way to the old commercial centre where they finally find the club.

5. Zoe doesn't really want a drink, but has a lobotomizer because she doesn't want to appear boring to her friends.

6. Ned gives the bouncer the entrance fee in coins.

7. Inside the *Blue Moon*, the music is very loud and there is a lot of smoke.

8. Zoe thinks Rawhampton is worse than she had imagined because people look at her and she cannot bear their cold eyes.

9. Larry notices that the Chippies can get in without paying and complains.

Correct order:

While-reading assignments (pp. 22 – 30)

1. p. 22

Daz and his friends try to ignore the Subbies in the Blue Moon to pretend indifference, but one Subby girl calls for Daz's attention. Why?

_____

2. pp. 23 – 24

Indicate the page(s) and line(s) where the text says that …

a) … Zoe is afraid of the Chippies.

b) …Zoe doesn't like the atmosphere at the *Blue Moon*.

c) … the drink makes Zoe feel relaxed.

d) … the Chippies forget their problems while dancing.

e) … Zoe falls in love at first sight with a Chippy boy.

f) … meeting the Chippy boy will bring about a radical change in Zoe and her life.

3. pp. 25 – 26

Explain why seeing Zoe gets Daz so confused.

_____

_____

_____

4. pp. 27 – 28

Briefly describe the problem and how it is solved.

_____

_____

_____

5. pp. 29 – 30

When the Subbies have left the *Blue Moon*, Mick gives Daz "this luck like I kick him in the teef" (p. 29, l. 25). What does he want to express by that look? Translate it into a few words or sentences.

_____

_____

While-reading assignments (pp. 31–45)

1. While reading pp. 31–36 find the following expressions and explain them within the context of the novel.

   a) to mope
   b) even
   c) puzzled look
   d) gorgeous
   e) to neglect sth.
   f) to be in a fix
   g) to stick your neck out for sb.
   h) to be out of the question

2. While reading p. 37 find out how Daz feels about having met Zoe.

3. While reading pp. 38–42 finish the following sentences with information from the text.

   a) Zoe feels imprisoned in Silverdale because _____

   b) If Zoe's dad were the government and there were a Chippy riot, he would _____

   c) Zoe finds herself with four different problems:

   1. _____
   2. _____
   3. _____
   4. _____

4. While reading p. 43 answer the following question: Why does Daz write the words "Dred gud, Subbys bad" so often in his maths book?

5. While reading pp. 44–45 keep the following definition of "brainwash" in mind and explain why Zoe has chosen this word to write across the lines she has to write for Miss Moncrieff. "[B]rainwash: to make someone believe something that is not true, by using force, confusing them, or continuously repeating it over a long period of time."

While-reading assignments (pp. 46 – 51)

1. While reading pp. 46 – 47 answer the following questions.

   a) In how far is Clint responsible for Del's death?

   _____

   _____

   b) What had Clint shown Daz when he was eleven years old?

   _____

   c) What happens to a Chippy being caught in an attempt to enter a suburb by cutting a fence?

   _____

   d) What makes the tunnel so dangerous?

   _____

   e) What is Daz's plan?

   _____

2. While reading pp. 48 – 49 decide whether the following statements are right or wrong.

	right	wrong
1. Miss Moncrieff is happy to see Zoe.		
2. Zoe is sure that Miss Moncrieff will rip up her lines.		
3. Miss Moncrieff believes Zoe when she says she doesn't know who wrote "brainwashing" on the thirteenth sheet.		
4. Zoe gets very angry and, as usual, answers her teacher's question in a very rude way.		

3. While reading pp. 50 – 51 find out how Daz plans to find Zoe.

   _____

   _____

   _____

   _____

Character and characterization in literature

A character is the representation of a person in a work of fiction (a novel, a play, or a film). The author creates the character and endows him or her with moral qualities that will determine his or her motivation.
A character may remain essentially stable or unchanged from the beginning to the end of a fictional text, or he or she may undergo a radical change, either through gradual development or as a result of an extreme crisis.

A flat character (also called a type, two-dimensional or static) is a simple, uncomplicated character that does not develop or change in the course of the action. The author presents him or her only in outline, without much individualizing detail. This kind of character can be described with a few adjectives.

A round character (also called dynamic or three-dimensional) is complex in temperament and motivation. The author presents him or her with detailed individual traits. He or she develops in the course of the story and changes his or her attitudes and values in the course of the action.

Characterization is the way the author presents his characters.
He may use a **direct or explicit** way of characterization (also called **telling technique**), and inform the reader (through the words of a narrator or other characters) directly what a character is like by using adjectives to describe his traits. Or he may use an **indirect or implicit** way of characterization (also called **showing technique**), and present the characters merely speaking and acting so that the reader has to draw his conclusions about the character's traits.

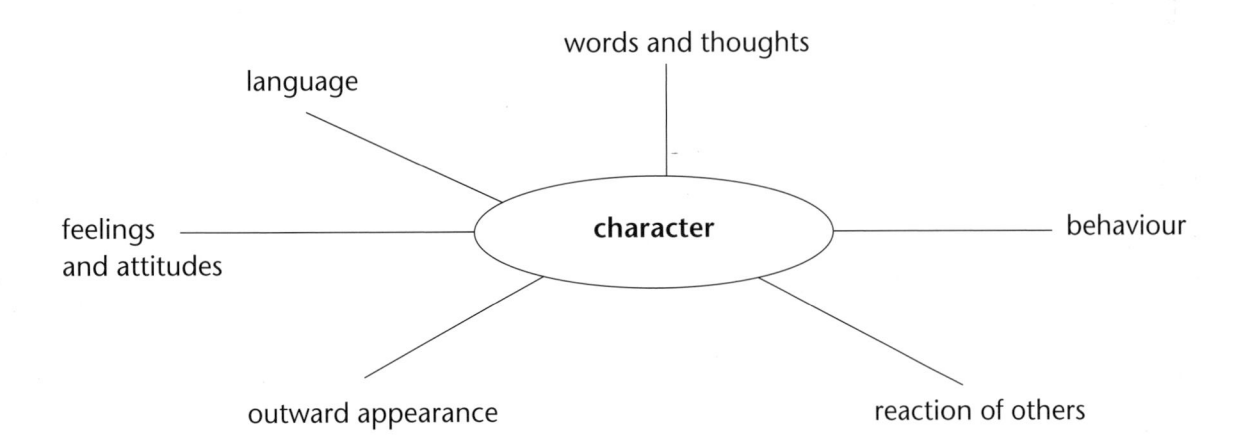

Aspects of characterization

- language
- words and thoughts
- feelings and attitudes
- behaviour
- outward appearance
- reaction of others

(all connected to: **character**)

Describing the behaviour of people

1. Find the corresponding nouns or adjectives for the words on the list. (Use a dictionary if necessary.)
2. Looking back at the first part of the novel (pp. 7–51), find three situations in which Zoe or Daz show the kind of behaviour described by the words from the list. Explain your decision and give evidence from the text.
3. Share your findings with a partner and compare.

adjective	noun	adjective	noun
impolite		insecure	
understanding			disrespect
	indifference	selfish	
rebellious			irresponsibility
	support	excited	
sympathetic		cool	
	self-confidence	protective	
helpless		caring	
hostile		mature	
	courage	proud	
anxious			envy

The following expressions might help you to form sentences.

Zoe's/Daz's behaviour in …

can be described as appears is is characterized by seems to be lacks is full of is dominated by shows no sign of can be explained by is (not) based on	rather completely totally quite predominantly	…	because … since … as …

Situation 1: _____
_____
_____
_____

Situation 2: _____
_____
_____
_____

Situation 3: _____
_____
_____
_____

Character profile

First name	
Last name	
Gender	
City of residence	
Age	
Family background	
Educational background	
Outward appearance	
Problems	
Goals	
Political views	
Personality traits	
Role in the novel	

Component 2

Love in the time of suppression

Auf den Seiten 52–104 erfährt der Leser, wie das erste Treffen der beiden verliebten Teenager unter vier Augen abläuft und welche Maßnahmen der Staat ergreift, um die beiden Bevölkerungsgruppen getrennt zu halten. Wir werden Zeuge, wie Zoe von der Sicherheitspolizei befragt wird, wie ihre beste Freundin mit ihrer Familie Silverdale verlassen muss, weil sie als Mitglieder einer Untergrundorganisation enttarnt wurden und wie in Zoe der Plan heranreift, ihre Familie zu verlassen und stattdessen mit Daz bei den *Chippies* zu leben.
Der Schwerpunkt der Arbeit in diesem *Component* liegt auf der Schulung der mündlichen Ausdrucksfähigkeit, die verstärkt in den Fokus der Richtlinien für den Englischunterricht aller Jahrgangsstufen gelangt. Sowohl in den *While-reading*-Aufgaben als auch in der Arbeit in der Klasse soll in dieser Sequenz intensiv die Mündlichkeit trainiert werden.

2.1 First meeting

Hausaufgabe zu dieser Stunde sind die *while-reading tasks* Zoe, p. 52 – Daz, p. 62 auf *Copy 13*, die zunächst besprochen werden. Die erste Aufgabe, der Dialog zwischen Zoe und ihrer Lehrerin, wird zuerst in Kleingruppen von drei Schülerinnen und Schülern besprochen. In der Gruppe einigt man sich darauf, welcher Dialog der beste ist. Danach finden sich sechs Schülerinnen und Schüler zusammen und ermitteln wiederum, welcher Dialog der beste ist. Je nach Größe des Kurses wird diese Neugruppierung wiederholt, bis man drei bis vier Dialoge als „Sieger" hat, die dann im Plenum vorgetragen werden.

> Your homework was to write a dialogue between Zoe and Miss Montcrieff. Get together with two more students and compare your dialogues – decide which one is best. Then get together in a group of six students and find out which dialogue is best.

Der Vorteil des Lautlesens in den Gruppen besteht darin, dass die Autoren oberflächliche Fehler in ihren Sätzen selbst erkennen und berichtigen können. Darüber hinaus erfährt ein laut vorgetragener Text eine höhere Wertschätzung und somit wird es bei regelmäßiger Anwendung der Methode zu einer sorgfältigeren Bearbeitung der Hausaufgaben kommen. Vor dem Vortrag der Dialoge wird besprochen, was man von einem solchen Vortrag erwartet. Die Kriterien werden in einem Tafelbild festgehalten.

> What is important when presenting your homework in class?

- speak clearly, loudly and slowly
- stand in front of the class
- try to use your voice to make your reading more interesting
- especially in a dialogue use "two voices" to make clear that two people are speaking
- ….

Nach dem Vortrag der besten Dialoge stellt sich die Frage, was die Schülerinnen und Schüler in Zoes Situation getan hätten. Es folgt eine Diskussion im Plenum.

What would you have done in Zoe's situation?

Bevor im Anschluss an diese Diskussion Freiwillige gesucht werden, die die Geschichte des Minotaurus mithilfe der *keywords* vortragen, werden gemeinsam Kriterien erarbeitet, nach denen man einen mündlichen Vortrag bewerten kann. Wiederum werden die Kriterien an der Tafel festgehalten.

What is important when giving an oral presentation?

- speak loudly, clearly and slowly
- address the audience
- keep eye contact with your audience
- use your notes
- do not read from a written text
- stand in front of the class
- try to use your voice to make your presentation more interesting
- practice your presentation at home to avoid long breaks and stuttering
- make sure that you include all necessary information
- …

Nach diesen Kriterien werden die *keywords* aus der Aufgabenstellung ebenfalls an die Tafel geschrieben. Ein Schüler oder eine Schülerin tragen vor, während ein weiteres Kursmitglied mit einer farbigen Kreide an der Tafel steht und die erwähnten keywords an der Tafel abhakt. Nach dem Vortrag wird im Plenum diskutiert, ob die Kriterien für eine mündliche Präsentation erfüllt wurden und es wird überprüft, ob alle Informationen genannt wurden. Die nächste Aufgabe (*matching exercise – vocabulary and definition*) wird im Plenum besprochen.

Lösungen zu *Copy 13*:
1 – e, 2 – f, 3 – d, 4 – g, 5 – a, 6 – h, 7 – c, 8 – b

Im Anschluss daran werden die grafischen Darstellungen des Tunnelsystems in der Klasse aufgehängt. Die Schülerinnen und Schüler gehen in kleinen Gruppen gemeinsam durch die Klasse und bleiben an einzelnen Bildern stehen, um die Ausführungen des „Künstlers" anzuhören. Auch hierbei wird auf die Einhaltung der Kriterien für mündliche Vorträge geachtet. Die Hausaufgabe zur nächsten Stunde ist, die Seiten Zoe, p. 63 – Daz, p. 75 zu lesen und die entsprechenden *While-reading*-Aufgaben auf **Copies 13** und **14** zu bearbeiten. Dabei sollen die Schülerinnen den *interior monologue* von Zoe, die Schüler den von Daz aufschreiben. Zu Beginn der nächsten Stunde werden die Schülerinnen und Schüler getrennt. Die Aufgabe besteht darin, die Hausaufgaben in den Gruppen vorzulesen und zu bestimmen, welche beiden Texte am besten sind. Wiederum dürfen Ergänzungen und Verbesserungen in der Gruppe vorgenommen werden. Im Anschluss daran werden je eine Schülerin und ein Schüler nach vorne gebeten, die ihre Texte nacheinander vortragen. Es wird wiederum Wert auf die in der vorherigen Stunde erarbeiteten Kriterien gelegt.

Component 2: Love in the time of suppression

Als Nächstes werden in einer Sammlungsphase die Aktivitäten bei einem ersten Date, die die Schülerinnen und Schüler in ihren Hausaufgaben zusammengetragen haben, an der Tafel notiert.

- go for a walk through the local park
- have an ice cream
- go together to a party at a mutual friend's house
- go to the cinema
- …

In einem kurzen Gespräch wird herausgearbeitet, dass diese Aktivitäten unter den Lebensbedingungen von Zoe und Daz nicht möglich sind. Diese Erkenntnis leitet zum nächsten Punkt der Hausaufgabe über – der mündlichen Präsentation der äußeren Lebensumstände der beiden Protagonisten. Auch hier kommen zwei bis drei Schülerinnen und Schüler zu Wort.
Die *Right-or-wrong*-Übung wird im Plenum besprochen.

Lösungen zu *Copy 14*:

1. wrong (nine o'clock)	2. right	3. right	4. wrong (they are warned)
5. wrong (note for Zoe)	6. right	7. wrong (Cal wants him to stay away from the tunnel)	8. right

Nach der Besprechung dieses Teils des Romans ist die Hausaufgabe, Zoe, S. 75 – Zoe, S. 97 zu lesen und die *While-reading*-Aufgaben auf *Copies 15* und *16* zu bearbeiten.

2.2 Domestic security

Um den Inhalt der Seiten 75 – 83 zu rekapitulieren, werden die Schülerinnen und Schüler aufgefordert, paarweise ihre Lösung der *scrambled summary* zu vergleichen. Nach dieser vorbereitenden Phase wird die *summary* im Plenum vorgetragen, wobei jeder Kursteilnehmer einen Satz vorliest.

Lösungen zu *Copy 14*:

11 – 3 – 8 – 1 – 9 – 6 – 2 – 10 – 4 – 7 – 5

Im Anschluss an diese Zusammenfassung werden Kleingruppen von drei bis vier Schülerinnen und Schülern gebildet, die eine szenische Lesung des Interviews, das Pohlmann mit Zoe führt, einüben. Es wird besonders Wert darauf gelegt, dass Mimik und Körpersprache der Akteure zum Text passen.

> In groups of three or four play out the scene of Pohlman's interview (p. 78, l. 21 – p. 81, l. 18). Act your part as convincingly as possible – watch your body language and your facial expressions.

Nach der Präsentation von ein bis zwei Gruppen wird im Plenum besprochen, wie sich Pohlman und Zoe in dieser Szene fühlen. Die Schülerinnen und Schüler werden aufgefordert, passende Adjektive an der Tafel zu sammeln. Dabei dürfen gerne Lexika benutzt werden.

Zoe	Pohlman
scared, frightened, fearful, alarmed nervous, worried, intimidated, excited …	confident, calm, cool, composed, self-assured, cool, dispassionate, casual …

Wie in allen totalitären Systemen wird auch die *Domestic security* ausführliche Dossiers über auffällige Mitglieder der Gesellschaft anlegen. Im Anschluss an die Besprechung der Vernehmungsszene sollen die Schülerinnen und Schüler nun ein solches Dossier für Zoe schreiben, das Pohlman nach dem Interview anlegt. Bevor diese Schreibaufgabe bearbeitet wird, werden an der Tafel (oder einem OHP) die Aspekte gesammelt, die für dieses Dossier relevant sind.

> Imagine you are Lieutenant Pohlman. After your interview with Zoe you go back to your office and write a file about Zoe. Which aspects will your file include?

Nach einer kurzen Ideensammlung wird den Schülerinnen und Schülern **Copy 17** ausgeteilt, das in Partnerarbeit bearbeitet werden soll. Als Hausaufgabe sollen die Ergebnisse dieser Partnerarbeit in Form eines mündlichen Berichts über die verdächtige Zoe May Askew, den Pohlman seinem Vorgesetzten geben muss, vorbereitet werden.

Die folgende Stunde beginnt mit dem Vortrag einiger der Berichte, die Pohlmann über Zoe angefertigt hat. Ein kurzes Gespräch im Plenum nach jedem Bericht evaluiert, inwiefern die Kriterien für mündliche Vorträge eingehalten wurden.

Danach werden in Kleingruppen von vier bis fünf Schülern die *notes* verglichen, die Zoe an Daz geschrieben hat. In den Gruppen werden Fehler berichtigt und es soll entschieden werden, welche *note* vorgelesen wird. In denselben Kleingruppen wird auch die nächste Aufgabe (*What are they thinking?*) besprochen. Im Plenum wird je ein Zitat mit möglichen Gedanken besprochen.

Nachdem so der Inhalt des Kapitels rekapituliert worden ist, wird das Thema *point of view* bearbeitet.

Lösungsvorschlag zu *Copy 17*:

Domestic security

Suspect Nr. 34 67 90 – BVF x 90

Name	Zoe Askew
Address	Rosewood Street 24 567189 Silverdale
Date of interview	5th August 2035
Reason for interview	Zoe Askew has come to our attention because her teacher, Miss Moncrieff, has called us after Zoe handed in a suspicious piece of homework. The suspect has written "brainwashing" in large letters on her extra assignment. Also we have heard that students call her "Chippy-lover".

Component 2: Love in the time of suppression

Impressions	• Zoe appears to be a headstrong and suspicious student. • She still is allowed to meet her friend Tabitha Wentworth. • She seems to hold something back; I do not know, yet, what it is. • She wants the comfort of Siverdale for everyone!
Recommendations for future action	• Keeping an eye on Zoe Askew seems to be necessary. • It has not become clear why she has written that word on her homework. • She holds dangerous views so we should keep tabs on her.
Possible further suspects	• Tabby Wentworth is already taken care of • Zoe's parents and other family members must be watched closely.

Who is telling the story of Daz and Zoe?

Die Antwort, dass es zwei Erzähler gibt, die abwechselnd die Geschichte erzählen, liegt auf der Hand. Falls der Begriff des *first-person narrators* im Kurs noch nicht bekannt wird, wird er an die Tafel geschrieben und es wird gebeten, dass „Beweise" für einen solchen Erzähler angeführt werden.

Can you prove that there is a first-person narrator?

Bereits im ersten Paragraph auf S. 85 findet man „I" und „me". Es schließt sich die Frage an, welche anderen Erzähler die Schülerinnen und Schüler kennen.

What other narrators of novels do you know?

- third-person narrator
- omniscient narrator

Im Unterrichtsgespräch wird geklärt, was der Unterschied zwischen diesen beiden und dem *first-person narrator* ist. Als Zusammenfassung dieses Gesprächs wird im Anschluss an die Besprechung **Copy 18** verteilt und gemeinsam gelesen, damit die Schülerinnen und Schüler eine Grundlage für die folgende Schreibaufgabe haben.
Wiederum wird der Kurs in drei Kleingruppen geteilt: Jeder Gruppe wird eine der Aufgaben 1–3 auf **Copy 18** zugewiesen. Die genannten Seiten müssen nicht komplett umgeschrieben werden, aber es sollte so viel Text produziert werden, dass der Unterschied zwischen dem Ausgangstext und der Schülerversion deutlich wird und von den Kleingruppen benannt werden kann. Lösungshinweise für diesen Vergleich finden sich in der dritten Spalte der Tabelle (*effect on the reader*). Abschließend wird diskutiert, weshalb der Autor sich für die Erzählperspektive entschieden hat.

Lösungsvorschläge zu *Copy 18*:

Gruppe 1 (omniscient narrator)

Zoe's parents were really worried by the visit of the DS and so it was difficult for Zoe to get away from home. She had hoped to be able to leave home under the pretence of visiting Tabby and spending some time at her house listening to music. She needed to be out of the house by four thirty because she wanted to meet Daz at the end of the tunnel at seven o'clock.

At twenty-five past four she called out, "Mum, I'm going over to Tabby's. I won't be late." ….

Gruppe 2 (third-person narrator, Zoe)

Zoe wasn't scared of any monsters but still it was scary in the tunnel. What if DS had decided to patrol the area? What if she was found? What if they watched her? What could she say if stopped and interrogated? Zoe was nervous to say the least.

Fortunately, she didn't meet anybody and started her trip into the tunnel without any problem. …

Gruppe 3 (third-person narrator, Daz)

Daz was four minutes early for his date with Zoe. He was still hurting from the beating he had had. His face was badly bruised. When Zoe said, "I'm sorry. This whole thing is so dangerous for you. You shouldn't have come." he only laughed and told her that he really had no choice. He loved her too much. They cuddled for a little while and he forgot time and all the dangers they were in and all the obstacles that lay ahead of them. He was happy. ….

Als Hausaufgabe zur nächsten Stunde sollen die Schülerinnen die Seiten 84 – 97 lesen und die entsprechenden *While-reading*-Aufgaben auf **Copy 15** bearbeiten.

2.3 Choices

Die Schülerinnen und Schüler werden aufgefordert, sich in Kleingruppen ihre *notes*, die sie in der Hausaufgabe (*Copy 15:* Daz, p. 84) geschrieben haben, gegenseitig vorzulesen und zu entscheiden, welcher Text der beste ist. Nach dieser Entscheidung versuchen sie, eventuelle Fehler zu korrigieren und inhaltliche Ergänzungen vorzunehmen. Danach sollen sie den besten Text im Plenum vortragen.

Im Anschluss an diese Vorträge wird die Tabelle zu Zoe p. 85 besprochen, in der die Schülerinnen und Schüler die Gedanken der Charaktere, die die Sätze sagen, aufschreiben sollten.

Lösungsvorschläge zu *Copy 15:*

Quotation	Thoughts
"You're not going any place, young lady."	What does she think she is doing? I'm glad that Pohlman hasn't been back! (p. 85)
"She's right, Gerald – she can't just not show up."	Oh no, we're in enough trouble as it is – I don't want to have a discussion with the Wentworths. (p. 86)
"What the heck happened to you?"	Oh, my God – he looks like something the cat dragged in – did they see him – did he have a narrow escape? (p. 87)
"What's happened to Tabby, Mrs Corrigan?"	Why does nobody say what's wrong? Is Tabby sick? Has she had an accident? (p. 91)
"What are you doing here, Zoe?"	Why isn't she at school? Has she already heard what's happening here? (p. 93)

Quotation	Thoughts
"Don't talk that way, Zoe."	What's the matter with Zoe – she sounds so desperate! (p. 94)
"I wish I was coming with you."	That could be a solution – run away – get out of this difficult situation – be rid of Pohlmann (p. 95)
"Your father sold the house."	I know that Zoe will be shocked – but it really is the best we could do! (p. 96)

Nach der Besprechung der Hausaufgabe sollen die Schülerinnen und Schüler laut den Text Daz, p. 98 lesen und die entsprechende Aufgabe auf *Copy 16* lösen. Sie schreiben in Einzelarbeit einen Dialog, den sie dann mit einem Partner vergleichen. Erneut wird von ihnen selbst entschieden, welcher Dialog der bessere ist.

> Compare your dialogues with your partner and decide which one is best. Correct mistakes and add anything you would like to have in the dialogue, too. Practise presenting your dialogue to the class.

Im Anschluss an die Partnerarbeit werden einige Dialoge im Plenum vorgetragen und kurz besprochen.
Als Hausaufgabe werden die folgenden Seiten bis Seite 104 gelesen und die entsprechenden Aufgaben auf *Copy 16* gelöst.

An der Tafel werden dann die Möglichkeiten notiert, die Zoe hat, nachdem sie erfahren hat, dass ihre Eltern aus Silverdale wegziehen wollen.

Mögliche Lösungen Zoe, p. 99 *(Copy 16)*:

- She can try to persuade her parents not to leave Silverdale.
- She can live with her grandma.
- She can try to live with Daz.
- She can run away from home.
- ….

Den Schülerinnen und Schülern wird dann Zeit gegeben, ihre vorbereiteten Vorträge zu überarbeiten. Wiederum wird eine Schülerin oder ein Schüler gebeten, an die Tafel zu kommen und die im Schülervortrag genannten Ideen mit farbiger Kreide abzuhaken. Erneut wird bei der Besprechung der Vorträge darauf geachtet, ob die Kriterien für mündliche Vorträge beachtet worden sind.

Die inhaltliche Zusammenfassung von Daz p. 102 *(Copy 16)* könnte so lauten:

> Daz has a gun with 5 bullets that belonged to his dead brother Del. He muses about the fact that he once wanted to kill Subbies with it and now tries to save the Wentworths who are in danger of falling victim to an ambush. His mom does not know where he is going.

Component 2: Love in the time of suppression

Für die Besprechung der letzten Aufgabe *(Copy 16)*, werden zwei Schüler oder Schülerinnen gebeten, an die Tafel zu kommen und die Argumente für und gegen Zoes Weglaufen in einer Tabelle zu notieren.

for running away	against running away
• can't imagine what it would be like to live without communicating with Daz • would never again see Daz • impossible to live without Daz • impossible to live without daily contact to her grandma	• there are many difficulties • she must get out of Silverdale on her own – without using the tunnel • she doesn't know how to live as a Chippy • dependent on Daz – doesn't know if he can help her • doesn't know what Daz's mom will say • will never again see her family

Nach der Sammlung der Argumente finden sich die Schülerinnen und Schüler in Dreiergruppen zusammen. Eine Schülerin oder ein Schüler steht zwischen zwei anderen und spielt Zoe. Auf je einer Seite steht ein guter Engel und ein böser Teufel. Die Engel und Teufel reden abwechselnd auf Zoe ein und versuchen, sie auf ihre Seite zu ziehen. Dabei müssen die Schülerinnen und Schüler selbst entscheiden, welche Position sie dem Teufel oder Engel zuschreiben. Neben den Argumenten, die an der Tafel gesammelt wurden, dürfen die Engel und Teufel natürlich auch eigene Ideen verwenden. Im Anschluss an die Erarbeitung werden die Ergebnisse einzelner Gruppen vorgetragen. Im Plenum wird dann diskutiert, wie Zoe sich entscheiden wird und wie die Zoes der Klasse sich entschieden hätten.

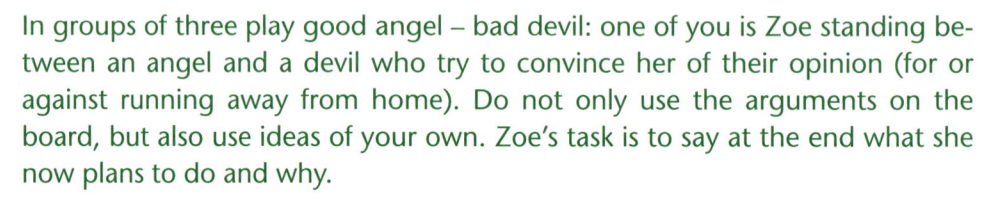

> In groups of three play good angel – bad devil: one of you is Zoe standing between an angel and a devil who try to convince her of their opinion (for or against running away from home). Do not only use the arguments on the board, but also use ideas of your own. Zoe's task is to say at the end what she now plans to do and why.
>
> What do you think Zoe will do?

Nach dieser inhaltlichen Erarbeitung des "Kapitels" sollen die Schülerinnen und Schüler nun den Text sprachlich analysieren. Abhängig vom Kenntnisstand der Klasse müssen die gängigen Stilmittel zunächst erläutert werden. *Copy 19* bietet hier eine Grundlage. Die Hausaufgabe besteht dann darin, dass die Schülerinnen und Schüler auf Seiten 103 und 104 Beispiele für die genannten Stilmittel finden.

> Re-read pages 103 and 104. Find different stylistic devices and mark them in your text.

In einem zweiten Schritt sollen die Schülerinnen und Schüler nun erörtern, welche Effekte die verschiedenen Stilmittel haben. Dazu wird die Klasse wiederum in Kleingruppen eingeteilt, die je ein bis zwei Stilmittel auf ihre Wirkung hin untersuchen. Die Ergebnisse dieser Arbeit werden dann im Plenum vorgestellt und alle Kursteilnehmer notieren sich die Vorschläge auf *Copy 19*.

Component 2: Love in the time of suppression

Lösungsvorschlag Copy 19:

stylistic device	definition	example	effect
alliteration	succession of words with the same initial sound	flights and freeways (p. 104, ll. 15/16) trash truck (p. 104, l. 20)	The effect of the alliteration of "flights and freeways" in this text is an emphasis on the fact that there is always a connection between the suburbs, but that there is no access to the inner city area.
anaphora	repetition of a word or group of words at the beginning of successive clauses	I thought about (p. 103, ll. 13/14) Would Daz's mother,…Would she… (p. 104, ll. 6/7)	This anaphora is connected with the tricolon and shows how insecure Zoe is and how much she worries about her future.
antithesis	a figure of speech in which sharply contrasting ideas are juxtaposed	dream and reality (p. 103, l. 22) here in Silverdale or a hundred miles away in Peacehaven (p. 104, ll. 12/13)	The numerous antitheses in this text passage point out that Zoe is full of doubts about what to do. She has to choose between two totally different lifestyles.
enumeration	the listing of words or phrases	First … Then… And then (pp. 103/04, ll. 26 – 9)	The enumeration of what she has to do to follow her plan through shows the reader how difficult and dangerous her plan is.
metaphor	a figure of speech in which an implied comparison is made between two unlike things that actually have something in common.	steely cold sky (p. 103, l. 23) the yawning chasm that lies between Veezaville and Chippyland (p. 104, l. 17)	The metaphor of the steely cold sky shows that even the natural environment is hostile towards her. The yawning chasm again underlines the supposedly insurmountable gap between Subbies and Chippies.
telling name	a name that draws attention to a feature typical of what it describes	Silverdale, Peacehaven	Telling names have a subconscious effect on the reader. Who would not want to live in a place called Peacehaven, especially after having been prosecuted by Domestic Security?
tricolon	a sentence with three clearly defined parts of increasing power (power of three)	Would Daz's mother be prepared to feed me? Would she be able to? And anyway, why should she? (p. 104, ll. 6-8)	The tricolon puts emphasis on the worries that torture Zoe in that situation.
question	often rhetorical question where no answer is expected because the answer is obvious	Then if I did get out, how would I live? (p. 104, l. 1)	The many questions in this excerpt reinforce the reader's impression that Zoe's emotions are in turmoil. She is not sure of what to do.

> You have found a number of stylistic devices in the text. Work in small groups and explain what effect these stylistic devices have.

Damit ist die Arbeit an **Component 2** abgeschlossen. Als Hausaufgabe zur nächsten Stunde werden die Seiten 105 bis 112 gelesen und die entsprechenden *While-reading*-Aufgaben auf *Copy 20* gelöst.

While-reading assignments (pp. 52 – 64)

Zoe, p. 52

Zoe is forced by her parents to apologize to her horrible teacher Miss Moncrieff. Having considered her only other option, suicide, and having rejected it, she realizes that she will have to do it like Galileo. Write the dialogue between Zoe and Miss Moncrieff.

Daz, p. 56

Daz uses a trick he learned about in school to find his way out of the tunnel system. Prepare an oral presentation about the myth of the Minotaur. The following key words can help you.

King	Minos	Crete	Daedalus	Athens	Prince	Theseus	Ariadne	ball of string

Look at the following websites for information:
- http://greece.mrdonn org/theseus.html
- http://www.pantheon.org/articles/m/minotaur.html
- http://www.qods-and-monsters.com/minotaur-greek-mythology.html

Zoe, p. 58

Match the words with their definitions.

1. to get kicked out of
2. to fraternize
3. insult
4. to stick up for
5. to bother
6. to look down your nose at
7. to associate with
8. to shake off

a) to annoy, worry or upset
b) to get rid of sth
c) to spend time with sb, especially people that sb else does not approve of
d) remark or action that is said or done in orwder to offend sb
e) to be made to leave
f) to behave in a friendly manner, especially towards sb that you are not supposed to be friendly with
g) to defend or support
h) to hold in contempt

Daz, p. 60

Having read Daz's description of the tunnel system that leads him from downtown to Silverdale, draw a map of that system. You may use symbols to point out dangerous or exciting places. Prepare a short oral presentation of your art work.

Zoe, p. 63 – Daz, p. 64

1. Explain why Zoe uses a back street to get home that afternoon.
2. You read about the two teenagers' feelings when they encounter each other for the second time in their lives. Write a short interior monologue for each of them at that moment – you may use the information from the book and add ideas of your own.

ZOE	DAZ
was waking home from school taking a back street when I suddenly saw someone climb out of a hole in the ground –	I had made it – I was crawling out of the hole at the other side of the fence when I saw her –

While-reading assignments (pp. 65 – 83)

Zoe, p. 65 – Daz, p. 70

1. Think of things you would do on a first date. Make a list of 5 activities.
2. In this part of the book the reader learns quite a lot about the way the suburbs are separated from the inner city area. Prepare an oral presentation of the means the government uses to keep these two places apart. Say how effective these means are in your opinion.

Zoe, p. 71 – Daz, p. 74

Right or wrong?

	right	wrong
1. There is a news bulletin at ten o'clock.		
2. Zoe is not bothered by the weather forecast.		
3. Zoe is very afraid that something bad has happened to Daz.		
4. In the local news the people of Silverdale are asked to help catch a dangerous man.		
5. Daz goes to the trash crew because he wants to get a job there.		
6. Daz manages to get a note on its way that will reach Zoe on Saturday.		
7. Mick and two of his friends beat up Daz because he tried to steal money from them.		
8. Cal is worried that the Subbies will now find the tunnel.		

Zoe, p. 75

Find the correct order of the sentences of this summary.

1. Zoe visits the Wentworths and is surprised when Tabby's father and not the maid opens the door.
2. Pohlman asks her about her trouble with Miss Moncrieff and confronts her with the fact that she is called "Chippy lover" at school.
3. Fortunately, her mum asks her to bring out a bag of trash.
4. After the police have left, Zoe's parents ask her about the interview.
5. Zoe's dad is afraid people will believe they are members of FAIR – the Fraternal Alliance for Integration through Reunification.
6. Zoe is afraid when she meets Lieutenant Pohlman from Domestic Security and has to talk to him because she thinks he is there because of her note to Daz.
7. Zoe's dad is sure that their life in Silverdale will not be the same anymore because they will be put under surveillance.
8. She exchanges her note for Daz's note.
9. Tabby behaves oddly and refuses to explain what's up.
10. When Zoe asks if she has done anything illegal Pohlman does not tell her, but he clearly warns her not to risk her safe and comfortable life in Silverdale.
11. It is Saturday and Zoe waits for the trash truck.

While-reading assignments (pp. 84–97)

Daz, p. 84

Write the note Zoe sends Daz.

Zoe, p. 85

What are they thinking?
Find the quotations in this part of the book and write down what the character saying this is thinking.

Quotation	Thoughts
"You're not going any place, young lady."	
"She's right, Gerald – she can't just not show up."	
"What the heck happened to you?"	
"What's happened to Tabby, Mrs Corrigan?"	
"What are you doing here, Zoe."	
"Don't talk that way, Zoe."	
"I wish I was coming with you."	
"Your father sold the house."	

While-reading assignments (pp. 98–104)

Daz, p. 98

In the *Blue Moon* Daz overhears a conversation and learns that Zoe's friends, the Wentworths, have been evicted from Pleasantville. It is obvious that some kind of robbery is planned. Write a dialogue:

- Who is talking?
- What are they saying about the Wentworths?
- What are they planning?

Zoe, p. 99

Think about the choices Zoe has when she finds out that her parents are moving to another suburb. Make a list and prepare an oral presentation saying also what you would do in her situation.

Daz, p. 102

Summarize the content of this part of the book in about fifty words.

Zoe, p. 103

Reading this part of the book, fill in the arguments Zoe runs through when contemplating what to do.

for running away	against running away

File on Zoe

Domestic security

Suspect Nr. 34 67 90 – BVF x 90

Name	
Address	
Date of interview	
Reason for interview	
Impressions	
Recommendations for future action	
Possible further suspects	

Narrator and point of view

Do not confuse the author with the narrator of a text. The author creates the narrator to tell his story so the narrator is a construction and not the same person as the author.
The author is outside of the story; the narrator is part of it.

Depending on the point of view the narrator has, there are three different narrative situations.

narrator	point of view	effect on reader
omniscient narrator	narrator is outside of the story, he knows and comments on everything	narrator leads readers through the story, readers are directly addressed but there is distance to the action
first-person narrator	limited point of view, narrator is either a minor character observing the action or a protagonist participating in the action	readers can identify with narrator but must also ask themselves if they can rely on what the narrator tells them
third-person narrator	limited point of view, tells the story from the point of view of one or several (shifting point of view) characters in the story	impersonal narrator so there is no direct contact, impression of being close to action, identification is made possible, readers must ask themselves if they can rely on narrator

1. Rewrite pp. 85/86 using an omniscient narrator.
2. Rewrite pp. 87–89 using a third-person narrator (Zoe).
3. Rewrite pp. 87–89 using a third-person narrator (Daz).
4. Compare the text of the novel with your new text.
5. Why does Robert Swindells use the two first-person narrators?

Stylistic devices

stylistic device	definition	example	effect
alliteration	succession of words with the same initial sound		
anaphora	repetition of a word or group of words at the beginning of successive clauses		
antithesis	a figure of speech in which sharply contrasting ideas are juxtaposed		
enumeration	the listing of words or phrases		
metaphor	a figure of speech in which an implied comparison is made between two unlike things that actually have something in common		
telling name	a name that draws attention to a feature typical of what it describes		
tricolon	a sentence with three clearly defined parts of increasing power (power of three)		
question	often rhetorical question where no answer is expected because the answer is obvious		

Component 3

A glimpse of hope in the desert

3.1 A flight into unknown territory

Die folgenden Unterrichtsstunden dienen der intensiven inhaltlichen Erarbeitung der Seiten 105 bis 155. Im weiteren Verlauf des Romans liegt der Schwerpunkt auf der Flucht Zoes aus den *suburbs*, ihrem anschließenden dortigen Versteckspiel, der dramatischen Konfrontation mit *Dred*-Mitgliedern und der Polizei und ihrer anschließenden Flucht zusammen mit Daz. Als durchgängige Hausaufgabe für die Arbeit in diesem *Component* wird das Ausfüllen eines *characterization grid* für Daz, Zoe und Grandma (**Copy 26**) gestellt. Die Erarbeitung des Inhaltes des letzten Teils des Buches erfolgt in vier Unterteilungen, die jeweils auf den *while-reading assignments* angegeben sind. Zu diesen ist in der Hausaufgabe jeweils ein *characterization assignment* angegeben. Nach dem letzten *characterization assignment* wird ein Erwartungshorizont abgedruckt. Während der Arbeit in *Component 1* wurde bereits der Auftrag erteilt, ein *character profile* **(Copy 12)** für Daz, Zoe oder Grandma mit den Informationen, die der erste Teil des Romans liefert, auszufüllen. Am Ende des **Component 3** werden die Schülerinnen und Schüler aufgefordert, das schon begonnene *character profile* mithilfe des vollständig ausgefüllten *characterization grid* zu vervollständigen.

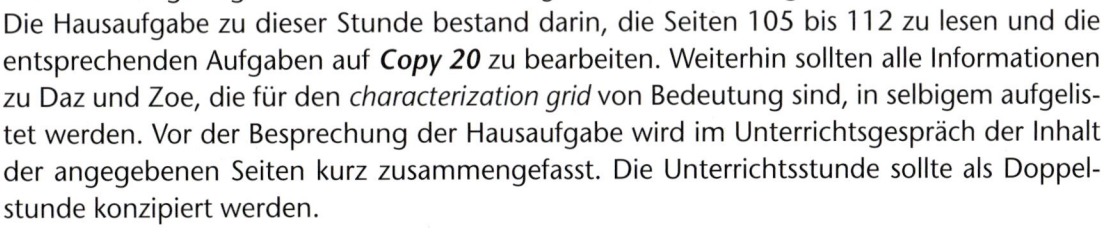

Die Hausaufgabe zu dieser Stunde bestand darin, die Seiten 105 bis 112 zu lesen und die entsprechenden Aufgaben auf **Copy 20** zu bearbeiten. Weiterhin sollten alle Informationen zu Daz und Zoe, die für den *characterization grid* von Bedeutung sind, in selbigem aufgelistet werden. Vor der Besprechung der Hausaufgabe wird im Unterrichtsgespräch der Inhalt der angegebenen Seiten kurz zusammengefasst. Die Unterrichtsstunde sollte als Doppelstunde konzipiert werden.

> Sum up the content of pp. 105 – 112 in your own words:
> Daz kills Pete because he wants to protect the Wentworths. Zoe plays truant because she needs to contemplate what to do. She flees from Silverdale hiding underneath a garbage truck.
>
> **Lösungsvorschlag zu Copy 20**: 1c; 2a; 3b; 4a; 5c.

Die Auseinandersetzung mit den Ereignissen auf den angegebenen Seiten wird in Form einer *Chessboard*-Aktivität durchgeführt.
Es wird eine große Karte für die Wand vorbereitet, die das Aussehen eines Schachbrettes mit hellen und dunklen Quadraten hat. Die hellen Quadrate sollen für die positiven Aspekte der zweigeteilten Gesellschaft, die dunklen entsprechend für die negativen stehen. Um die Gruppe einzustimmen, wird die Frage gestellt, wie man zum Beispiel das Thema *flight from the suburbs* einordnen würde und warum. Welche Konsequenzen hat die Entscheidung zu einer Flucht? Welche Vorteile ergeben sich für jemanden, der diese Entscheidung trifft?

> What do you think about an escape from the suburbs? Give reasons.
>
> - dangerous, last hope for lovers, crazy idea, giving up comfortable life for good …

Component 3: A glimpse of hope in the desert

What consequences does such an escape have?

- no reunion with family possible once you are gone, missing life, looked for by police / Domestic security …

What adventages do you see for someone who undertakes such an escape?

- hope for life in freedom, no more threats by Domestic security …

(Man folgt seinen individuellen Gefühlen und Neigungen, statt sich vom Staat alles aufoktroyieren zu lassen; man eröffnet sich die Chance, das Leben und die Menschen im anderen Teil des Staates kennenzulernen.) Welche Nachteile ergeben sich dagegen? (Man bringt sich und seine Familie in Gefahr; man stellt sich einer unsicheren, gefährlichen und ungewissen Zukunft.)
Man teilt die Klasse in vier Gruppen auf, von denen jeweils eine mit einem Viertel des Spielfeldes arbeitet. Die Gruppen bekommen beispielsweise folgende Themenanordnung:

Flight from the suburb area.
Obeying the rules of the state.
Expressing criticism openly.
Leaving the suburbs to go into a disco in the Chippy area.
Joining FAIR.
Staying in touch with suspicious people.

Die Aufgabe der Gruppe besteht nun darin zu entscheiden, ob jeder dieser Vorschläge gut oder schlecht ist, und ein Zitat aus dem Buch bzw. in den angegebenen Seiten zu finden, welches ihre Meinung unterstützt. Daraufhin schreibt die Gruppe die Vorschläge zusammen mit dem belegenden Zitat und der entsprechenden Lektüreseite auf ein Stück Papier, welches sie entweder auf ein helles oder ein dunkles Quadrat in ihrem Sektor heftet. Falls sie in einem Vorschlag sowohl positive als auch negative Aspekte sieht, kann sie jeweils ein Stück Papier mit den entsprechenden belegenden Zitaten sowohl einem hellen als auch einem dunklen Quadrat zuordnen. Nachdem alle Quadrate vollständig ausgefüllt worden sind, kommt es gewöhnlich zu einer lebhaften Diskussion aufgrund der Tatsache, dass die einzelnen Vorschläge von den jeweiligen Gruppen oft unterschiedlich eingestuft wurden.

Your task is to decide whether these activities are good or bad and to find a quote from the underlying pages or from the previous ones which supports your opinion. Then write the topic on a slip of paper, together with the supporting quote and page number, and pin it on to a light or a dark square in your sector of the chessboard. If you consider any topic to have both positive and negative aspects, you are allowed to pin it on both squares, with different supporting quotes.
When all four parts of the chart have been filled in, we will probably have a discussion resulting from the fact that topics have been placed on opposite squares by different groups.

Examples:

Flight from the suburb area.

⊕ I'd tried to imagine what it'd be like to be a hundred miles away from Daz, knowing for certain we were never going to meet again and not even able to communicate through notes. I couldn't do it. (p. 103, ll. 10 – 13)
⊖ I mean, what Subby in her right mind would choose to be a Chippy? (p. 111, ll. 16 f.)

Component 3: A glimpse of hope in the desert

Obeying the rules of the state.

- ⊕ ... And you've got the most important thing of all, which is security. You're safe in Silverdale, Zoe. Safe and snug. Nothing can touch you. Nothing can hurt you.
There are no hassles here. No problems.' He looked at me. 'Would you want to lose all that? Live outside? Is that what you want?' (p. 81, ll. 3 – 8)
- ⊖ Brainwashing. I am, because Grandma uses it all the time. She says half of what's on TV and in the papers is brainwashing, and she reckons a lot of what they teach us in school is brainwashing, too. (p. 44, ll. 16 –19)

Expressing criticism openly.

- ⊕ 'They're people, Dad. Some of them're probably nice if you know them.' (p. 39, ll. 5 f.)
- ⊖ 'Riot? I'd give 'em riot. I'd have a door-gunner in every 'copter and cream 'em.' He snorts. 'They'd think twice before they'd riot again, I can tell you.' (pp. 38 f., ll. 27 – 2)

Leaving the suburbs to go into a disco in the Chippy area.

- ⊕ ... I'm off down town tonight with some of the kids. We thought we'd get drunk, do a little coke, maybe dance with some of them husky Chippy guys. (p. 14, ll. 10 ff.)
- ⊖ The reason it's dangerous is, two reasons. First, you've got money and they don't, and they know you have it, and there's a lot of them and only a few of you. And second, they hate you anyway, cause you're a Subby and they'd as soon kill a Subby as look at him. (p. 10, ll. 23 – 26)

Joining FAIR.

- ⊕ An illegal, underground outfit whose members believe the world'd be a better place if we tore down our fences and invited the Chippies to come share our lifestyle. (p. 82, ll. 19 ff.)
- ⊖ 'We are moving, Zoe, but not through choice. We have to go tomorrow because –.' Her control snapped. She howled and threw her arms round me. 'They've kicked us out, Zoe, we can't stay here anymore.' (p. 93, ll. 12 –15)

Staying in touch with suspicious people.

- ⊖ 'Go away, Zoe. There's a cop out front. If they find you here they'll think you're one of us.' (p. 93, ll. 21 f.)
- ⊕ It was magic. It was. I know it sounds corny and all that, but you really do get so wrapped up in each other you forget everything else. I mean, the guy was risking his life just being there and we didn't even think about it. (p. 65, ll. 3 – 6)

Die Hausaufgabe zur nächsten Stunde besteht darin, die Seiten 113 bis 122 zu lesen und den *characterization grid* **(Copy 26)** weiter zu vervollständigen.

Die folgende Unterrichtsstunde sollte wiederum als Doppelstunde vorgesehen werden. Zunächst werden die Ergebnisse der Einträge in den *characterization grid* vorgetragen und verglichen. Als geeignet erweist sich eine Präsentation auf dem OH-Projektor, mit welchem das vorgegebene Raster auf Folie präsentiert und anschließend ausgefüllt wird. Falls der Unterrichtsraum über einen Beamer und Laptop verfügt, kann das vorgegebene Raster auch an der Tastatur ausgefüllt werden.

Component 3: A glimpse of hope in the desert

Im Anschluss daran wird der Inhalt der Seiten 113 bis 122 kurz zusammengefasst und dann die Aufgabe auf *Copy 21* in Einzelarbeit bearbeitet. Daraufhin wird das ausgefüllte Lösungsraster als Folie auf dem OH-Projektor präsentiert. Die von den Schülerinnen und Schülern eingesetzten Begriffe werden ebenfalls verglichen.

Sum up pages 113 to 122 in your own words.

Lösungsvorschlag:

Zoe leaves Silverdale under a garbage truck. She has only a vague idea of where Daz lives. On her way to the tallest block in town she meets a group of children who steal everything usable from a dead body. Finally, she arrives at Daz's apartment. He is overwhelmed at meeting her; his mother, however, is shocked to see a girl from the suburbs in her place. After a miserable night without the comforts of her old home, Daz leaves the apartment to meet a "guy".

Lösung zu *Copy 21*:

	A	B	C	D	E	F	G	H	I	J	K	L	M	N	O
1	m														n
2		o				s								o	
3			u				m					s		i	
4		s		n				o		q		t			
5		u		m	d				u		a				w
6		s		u				e		l				h	
7		p		d			a		o		d		e		
8		i		d		l		s	y			e			
9		c		y	i		e		x		z		r		
10		i		n		d			a	i			e		
11		o	g						l						d
12		u						y	a						
13		s						g							
14							c	o	r	p	s	e			
15						g	n	i	n	n	i	r	g		

1. The forest **smouldered** for days after the terrible fire.
2. A **galaxy** consists of millions of stars.
3. The assistant looked at the **mound** of papers on the desk.
4. The family was left in **desolation** after the earthquake in which their home was destroyed.
5. This story sounds somewhat **suspicious** to me.
6. The road into the forest looked extremely **muddy**.
7. This woman is always **grinning** at me as if she does not take me seriously!
8. When the children saw the **corpse**, they were terrified.
9. The animals were **squealing** out of panic.
10. The person spoke **wheezily** as if she was inflicted by some kind of breathlessness.

Der Schwerpunkt der Auseinandersetzung mit dieser Stelle liegt zunächst allgemein auf der Kategorie des dystopischen Romans. Die Schülerinnen und Schüler werden aufgefordert, ihrer Meinung nach typische Merkmale eines dystopischen Romans aufzulisten. Die Ideen und Vorschläge werden an der Tafel oder am OH-Projektor gesammelt. Anschließend wird zur Vertiefung *Copy 22* im Unterrichtsgespräch eingesetzt. Dabei können die bisher eingebrachten Ideen mit den Vorschlägen von *Copy 22* verglichen werden.

Im sich anschließenden Unterrichtsschritt werden die Schülerinnen und Schüler aufgefordert, nach der methodischen Vorgehensweise von *expert groups* herauszufinden, inwieweit die auf der *Copy 22* angegebenen Merkmale im vorliegenden Roman aufzufinden sind. Es werden drei Gruppen gebildet, von denen sich jeweils eine Gruppe mit einem von den Aspekten *characteristics of a dystopian society, types of dystopian controls* und *the dystopian protagonist* im Gruppengespräch auseinandersetzt. Die Mitglieder einer Gruppe erhalten jeweils ein gleichfarbenes Blatt, auf dem die Ergebnisse festgehalten werden.

> Group 1: What are the characteristics of a dystopian society?
> Group 2: What types of dystopian controls are there?
> Group 3: What can you say about the dystopian protagonist?

Anschließend werden Dreiergruppen gebildet, die sich aus jeweils einem Mitglied der drei anfangs gegebenen Gruppen zusammensetzen. Insofern stellen sich dann in einer Gruppe Gruppenmitglieder mit jeweils einem andersfarbigen Blatt dar. In diesen kleinen Gruppen tauschen sich die Mitglieder über die in ihrer jeweiligen Gruppe gesammelten Ergebnisse aus, sodass jede Schülerin und jeder Schüler alle Informationen erhalten kann.

Es ergibt sich zum Beispiel der im Folgenden dargestellte **Erwartungshorizont**:

Characteristics of a dystopian society in "Daz 4 Zoe"

- Propaganda is used to control the citizens of a society.
  - → assertion that life in the suburbs is comfortable, safe, and offering possibilities of education ("'Silverdale, right? … Is that what you want?'", pp. 80f., ll. 30 – 8)
  - → perception of Chippies as decrepit and cultureless underdogs ("There's us and there's them, … they don't want to work.", p. 9, ll. 4 –13)
- Information, independent thought, and freedom are restricted.
  - → after an incident of pointing at an enforcement of brainwashing in the Subby society, Zoe is put under heavy pressure ("I said, 'What she made me … Maybe I'll kill myself instead.", pp. 52f., ll. 24 –18)
- Citizens are perceived to be under constant surveillance.
  - → after the police have investigated into Zoe's reasons for her comment, the Askews fear to be under constant surveillance ("Ah, I turned to the window, … People know.", p. 96, ll. 22 – 27)
- Citizens live in a dehumanized state.
  - → the housing of the Chippy population is destitute; the kids' attitudes are respectless and violent ("The weeds thinned out … I just wanted out of there. p. 115, ll. 3 – 31; "The streets were cracked … but always there.", p. 117, ll. 1 –12)
- Citizens conform to uniform expectations. Individuality and dissent are suppressed.
  - → Tabby's family has to leave their home after it has been found out that they are members of FAIR ("'We are moving, Zoe, " … and they're wrong.'", p. 93, ll. 12 – 32)

Types of dystopian controls in "Daz 4 Zoe"

This dystopian work presents a world in which oppressive societal control and the illusion of a perfect society are maintained through bureaucratic and technological control:

- Bureaucratic control: Society is controlled by a mindless bureaucracy through a tangle of red tape, relentless regulations, and incompetent government officials.
  - → the suburbs have fences and lights and guards: if one wants to leave a suburb one has to pass a checkpoint with ID-check; they have to carry their ID all the time (p. 9; p. 15)
  - → there is a perimeter fence which is a double fence with a floodlit walkway being patrolled by security men; they have dogs and carry automatic weapons (p. 65)
  - → the department of Domestic Security spies on Subbies to make sure they stay in their area and shoots Chippies that transgress (p. 78)
- Technological control: Society is controlled by technology - through scientific means.
  - → there are TV cameras installed at the perimeter fence (p. 65) and there is remote surveillance (p. 72)
  - → the use of helicopters in the case of the search for a person

The dystopian protagonists Daz and Zoe

- feel trapped and are struggling to escape.
  - → because of their love for each other they want to stay together; therefore, each of them leaves their usual surroundings until Zoe's flight
- question the existing social and political systems.
  - → Zoe contradicts her dad on his judgement about Chippies ("'They're people, Dad. Some of them're probably … through the back of the neck.'", p. 39, ll. 5 –14)
- believe or feel that something is terribly wrong with the society in which they live.
  - → Zoe views her dad's harsh utterances about the attitude of Chippies critically (p. 9)
  - → Daz feels very ashamed of his circumstances and is aware of the discrepancy and injustice that is perceivable (p. 127)
  - → Daz wants to join Dred because he wants to take revenge for his brother, and he wants to take his anger about his life out on the Subbies (p. 12)
- help the audience recognize the negative aspects of the dystopian world through their own perspective.

Die Hausaufgabe zu dieser Stunde besteht darin, dass die Schülerinnen und Schüler in einer *Creative-writing*-Aufgabe versuchen, sich in die Situation von Zoes Mutter nach Zoes Flucht hineinzuversetzen. Zoes Mutter scheint nicht ganz so rigide und starr wie ihr Mann zu sein und Zoe bis zu einem gewissen Grad auch zu verstehen. In dieser Aufgabe kann ihre Haltung zwischen Verständnis für ihre Tochter und ihrer Einsicht in die Notwendigkeit der Anpassung an die äußeren Umstände herausgestellt werden. Als zweiter Teil der Hausaufgabe bietet sich an, dass die Schülerinnen und Schüler den *characterization grid* auf der Grundlage der Seiten 123 bis 134 weiter vervollständigen.

> Put yourself in the position of Zoe's mum. She has just discovered that Zoe has fled. Describe your thoughts and feelings that you have in this situation. Consider your care for and worry about your daughter and, on the other hand, your anger at her flight. After all, you have agreed to comply with the rules of the society you live in.

3.2 Adventures in the unknown territory culminating in "High Noon"

Am Anfang der folgenden Unterrichtseinheit, die ebenfalls als Doppelstunde konzipiert werden sollte, werden zunächst einige Versionen der Hausaufgabe vorgelesen. Die Schülerinnen und Schüler werden vorher aufgefordert, diese nach den Kriterien Glaubwürdigkeit, Originalität und Überzeugungskraft zu beurteilen. Sie sollen nun über die beste bzw. die besten der vorgelesenen Versionen abstimmen, die dann zum Beispiel in Form einer Wandzeitung aufgehängt werden könnte.

Die dem *characterization grid* zugrunde liegenden Seiten 123 bis 134 eignen sich in ihrer Kürze, von den Schülern selbstständig und kooperativ (zumindest für einige Abschnitte) mit der Methode des *paired reading and thinking* (wechselseitiges Lesen und Erklären) erschlossen zu werden. Dazu bilden die Schüler Lesetandems, in denen je ein stärkerer Schüler mit einem schwächeren zusammenarbeitet. Der Text wird in folgende Sinnabschnitte unterteilt:

1. p. 123, l. 1 – p. 124, l. 30
2. p. 125, l. 1 – p. 126, l. 10
3. p. 127, l. 1 – p. 128, l. 7
4. p. 129, l. 1 – p. 130, l. 21
5. p. 130, l. 22 – p. 131, l. 8
6. p. 131, l. 9 – p. 132, l. 14
7. p. 132, l. 15 – p. 133, l. 17
8. p. 133, l. 18 – p. 143, l. 9

Die Schüler gehen abschnittsweise wie folgt vor:

> **Paired reading and thinking instructions**
>
> 1. Each person needs a copy of the reading material.
> 2. Partners sit next to each other.
> 3. Each person reads the first part alone.
> 4. One person reads this part again quietly to the partner.
> 5. The other partner corrects any mistakes in pronunciation, then retells the main points.
> 6. The reader asks questions about anything that is unclear and corrects or adds ideas. Both ask a few more questions and talk about the reading.
> 7. Switch roles and continue.
> 8. At the end talk about what you have read.
>
> (from: Grieser-Kindel, Christin/Henseler, Roswitha/Möller, Stefan: Method Guide – Methoden für einen kooperativen und individualisierenden Englischunterricht in den Klassen 5 – 12. Paderborn: Schöningh 2009, p. 126)

Da die von Daz präsentierten Abschnitte in einem *slang English* geschrieben sind, entfällt in diesen Abschnitten die Korrektur der falschen Aussprache. Jedoch können die Lesetandems ähnlich wie im ersten *Component* beschrieben vorgehen und die von Daz gesprochenen Abschnitte in der folgenden Weise bearbeiten:

Die jeweiligen Paare schreiben den Text von Daz in Partnerarbeit in korrektem Englisch auf und schreiben ihn anschließend wiederum in *standard English* um.

> Rewrite Daz's text first in correctly spelt English and finally convert it into standard English.

Das kann auch arbeitsteilig geschehen, damit nicht zu viel Zeit mit dieser Aufgabe verbracht wird. Die Analyse von Daz' Sprache entfällt an dieser Stelle, da diese den Rahmen sprengen würde. Bei dieser Aktivität sollte jedem Lesetandem ein Wörterbuch zur Verfügung stehen. In einer Plenumsphase berichten die Schüler, worüber sie gesprochen haben, und tauschen ihre Gedanken aus.

Component 3: A glimpse of hope in the desert

> What did you talk about? Share your ideas with the class.

Wahrscheinlich werden sie Zoes Unbehagen im Apartment von Daz' Mutter, die Schwierigkeiten der Kommunikation zwischen ihnen, Daz' Bitten an Mr James, Zoe zu einem Versteck zu verhelfen, ihre Eindrücke des Verstecks im Keller und anschließend die Unterbringung auf dem Dachboden der Schule thematisiert und kommentiert haben. Zum Abschluss der Arbeit zu den zugrunde liegenden Seiten 123 bis 134 können die Fragen auf *Copy 23* noch in Partnerarbeit gelöst werden.

> **Lösungsvorschlag zu *Copy 23*:**
>
> 1. He feels bad because he realizes that they have nothing that Zoe likes.
> 2. She thinks Zoe should have brought robust clothes and shoes instead of food.
> 3. There is no running water, no washing-up liquid and no tea towel. The water has to be taken down from the raintank on the roof.
> 4. They are looking for Zoe because she has run away.
> 5. The worst feeling for him is feeling ashamed of his own home.
> 6. He asks a favour of him: if he can hide Zoe for a short while.
> 7. Her hiding place under a furnace is very difficult to get into and is hardly recognizable.
> 8. She does not know how long she can stay in the hiding place in the school; she is afraid Daz and his mother will be caught if somebody finds her, and she becomes aware of the filthy circumstances in which she must live now.
> 9. That way she looks less like a Subby and therefore less suspicious.
> 10. She asks him if he could get a message to her parents, but he declines because, in that case, he would be arrested and forced to tell them where she is hiding.

Die Hausaufgabe zur nächsten Stunde besteht darin, die Seiten 135 bis 155 gründlich zu lesen und sich Stichpunkte für eine Zusammenfassung zu machen.
Die folgende Unterrichtsstunde sollte wieder als Doppelstunde konzipiert werden. Am Anfang der Stunde wird zunächst der Inhalt der Seiten 135 bis 155 zusammengefasst.

> **Sum up pages 135 – 155 in your own words.**
>
> **Lösungsvorschlag:**
>
> The police search the apartment but do not find anything. Daz is threatened because he has killed Pete. Zoe leaves her hiding place to wash. Daz is worried because not only the police but also Dred are after him. Zoe manages to flee from the school building. In a showdown Zoe and Daz manage to escape to a place pointed out by Grandma.

Im Anschluss daran wird die *While-reading*-Aufgabe *(Copy 24)* zu den letzten Seiten des Buches in Partnerarbeit bearbeitet. Eine Schülerin oder ein Schüler ergänzen gleichzeitig am OH-Projektor auf einer speziell vorbereiteten Folie ohne Interpretationseinträge oder am Laptop, welches mit einem Beamer verbunden ist, geeignete Schülerlösungen.

Lösungsvorschlag zu *Copy 24:*

Quotation	Interpretation
1. you can see by his face he finks he got his dirty little pause on the peanuts alreddy. (p. 135, ll. 5ff.)	The kid thinks that it does not take much to prove Daz's guilt, which will result in a reward for him.
2. I got that rest, because it was going to be a busy day. To say the least. (p. 139, ll. 21f.)	This is a slight understatement, because the day will not only be busy, but full of dangerous and difficult situations.
3. Yea, well – they luck lyke thay mean biznis, know wot I mean? (p. 140, l. 12)	The guys were serious about their enquiries and have a strong intention of finding Daz. They are mad at him for not joining Dred.
4. Now Wentworth's out and she's back up the sharp end at the age of one hundred and four. (p. 142, l. 28 to p. 143, l. 1.)	Despite her age she is willing to take the responsibility and face the difficulties involved.
5. Daz, supported by Mick and Smithy, was still on his feet. (p. 153, ll. 5f.)	The bullet did not hit or hurt Daz, but apparently somebody else has been hit.

Der Schwerpunkt der Auseinandersetzung mit dem letzten Teil des Buches liegt auf dem Verfassen eines Artikels, der in einer Zeitung, die in den *suburbs* gedruckt und verbreitet wird, geschrieben sein könnte. Das Thema ist das Verschwinden von Zoe, deren Spuren sich im Augenblick verlieren, und Überlegungen zu möglichen Verflechtungen mit Bewohnern aus der *Chippy-area*. Alle bisherigen Auffälligkeiten, die sie gezeigt hat, können mit einbezogen werden. Dabei können verschiedene Perspektiven des Schreibers, eines entfernten Beobachters, eingenommen werden: Zum einen kann eine kritische Haltung im Zentrum stehen, die ihr Verschwinden verurteilt und sie eines subversiven Verhaltens bezichtigt. Zum anderen kann eine wohlwollendere Haltung Zoe gegenüber eingenommen werden, die ihr Verschwinden als Ausdruck jugendlicher Hitzköpfigkeit und Unbedarftheit wertet.

Dazu wird zunächst **Copy 25** verteilt und gemeinsam laut gelesen, um die Lerngruppe mit der *text form* des *newspaper article* vertraut zu machen, die den Schülerinnen und Schüler unter Umständen noch nicht bekannt ist. Danach erhalten die Schülerinnen und Schüler Gelegenheit, selbst in Einzelarbeit einen *newspaper article* über das Verschwinden Zoes zu verfassen. Neben der objektiven Berichterstattung sollte in jedem Fall ein, wie oben dargestellt, wertender Kommentar eingeflochten werden.

> You are the reporter of a newspaper published in the suburbs of the society described in "Daz 4 Zoe". Write a newpaper article of not more than 400 words about the disappearance of the 14-year-old girl, Zoe, whose whereabouts cannot be traced. Mention her previous conspicuity at school and the ensuing reactions of her parents. Take into consideration various explanations about her behaviour.

Component 3: A glimpse of hope in the desert

Möglicher Lösungsvorschlag:

Missed girl an accomplice of FAIR?

Reasons for pupil disappearing can only be guesswork

It has been three days since Mr and Mrs Askew from Silverdale informed the police that their only daughter, Zoe, did not come home from school on September 14. On that day they were preparing their move to Peacehaven and were busy taking care of their final preparations for the move. As every day, their daughter Zoe took her bike to cycle to school. She had her regular schoolbag with her and was dressed inconspicuously.

Her parents are outraged and are desperate for a sign of life from their daughter. A thorough search has started and several people, among them some friends of Zoe's, have been interviewed about her possible whereabouts. Her mother stated that her daughter was "very dear" to her and that she was thinking of her day and night.

However, there are some suspicions that Zoe May Askew has connections to circles that consider harming the stable structure of our society. So, for example, the head of her school reported an incident in which she had written a subversive comment on a paper due for one of her teachers. Secondly, an undisclosed pupil from the same school gave out that on at least one occasion the girl had been "Chippying", i.e. leaving her secure area for a short ride into the Chippy district. Finally, her parents were preparing to move to Peacehaven because they did not feel comfortable anymore due to their daughter's doings.

Everybody in this area knows how dangerous the situation in the Chippy district is and how unpredictable the inhabitants are. Their style of life is completely averse to ours and they do not respect and appreciate the same values as we do. If we want to keep our security, safety and the high standard of living that we are enjoying, we have to stay away from that area and from their inhabitants. We do not want to ruin our very foundation, do we? If the girl is actually involved in the doings of the subversive FAIR-organization whose aim is to treat the Chippy people as equals and to improve their living conditions, then she can only be looked upon as completely misguided. A possible involvement in or support of the organization can only be ascribed to her immaturity and headlessness typical of young people of that age.

If all this is the explanation for Zoe's disappearance, once she is found it should be made very clear to her that she was deeply misled. She should have to face severe and harsh consequences!

Als erster Teil der Hausaufgabe soll der Artikel zu Ende verfasst werden. Der zweite Teil der Hausaufgabe besteht darin, den *characterization grid* auf der Grundlage der Seiten 153 bis 155 zu Ende auszufüllen.

In der folgenden Doppelstunde liegt das Hauptgewicht auf der Arbeit mit den Ergebnissen des *characterization grid*. Nachdem dieser auf der Grundlage der Lektüre der Seiten 105 bis zum Ende des Buches ausgefüllt wurde, sollen die Schülerinnen und Schüler im ersten Unterrichtsschritt die Eintragungen in den *characterization grid* nun für die endgültige Erstellung eines *character profile* für Daz oder Zoe verwenden. Dabei wird die schon im ersten

Component 3: A glimpse of hope in the desert

Component teilweise ausgefüllte *Copy 12* aus *Component 1*, die eine Struktur für ein *character profile* vorgibt, vervollständigt. Die Schülerinnen und Schüler bearbeiten diese Aufgabe in Partnerarbeit. Um allen Schülerinnen und Schülern eine fundierte Grundlage zu geben, wird ein Lösungsvorschlag des ausgefüllten *characterization grid* per Laptop und Beamer an die Wand geworfen. Nachdem die *character profiles* erstellt worden sind, werden sie anschließend in Form einer Wandzeitung an der Wand befestigt. Die Schülerinnen und Schüler schauen sich die Ergebnisse in einem Rundgang an, vergleichen sie und geben anschließend ihre Eindrücke wieder. Dabei kann man sich auf eine Rangfolge der drei oder mehr besten Ergebnisse einigen.

Im Folgenden werden ein Erwartungshorizont für den *characterization grid* *(Copy 26)* und jeweils einer für ein *character profile (Copy 12)* für Zoe, Daz und Grandma angegeben.

Als abschließende Aufgabe bei der Bearbeitung des Romans wird jetzt im Plenum noch einmal der Prolog des Romans (A True Story, p. 5) gemeinsam laut gelesen.

> Explain the meaning of this true story at the beginning of Daz 4 Zoe.
> - It is more important to save old people than palm trees.
> - Palm trees are an adornment and amenity; they are not necessary parts of our lives.
> - A society that puts trees before people is in real danger of losing touch with reality.
> - …

Mögliche Lösungsvorschläge für *character profile (Copy 12)* und *characterization grid (Copy 26)*:

First name	Darren "Daz"
Last name	Barraclough
Gender	male
City of residence	London – city centre where the "Chippies" live
Age	15
Family background	lives with his depressive mother in a shabby and dirty apartment without electricity and running water in the city centre of London in a high-rise building; his brother Del was killed at the age of 15 because he belonged to the organization "Dred"
Educational background	attends a school in the city centre which is only for "Chippy" children and where the level of education is low
Outward appearance	he has wild, greasy-looking hair and often wears a beat-up leather jacket
Problems	he lives with his depressive mother; he falls in love with Zoe who lives in the suburbs; as they cannot meet without danger Zoe decides to flee to his part of town and hide in his apartment, which forces him to find a safe place for her to hide; he gets in trouble with some Dred members because after a guy called Pete hurt him badly he kills him and the Dred members promise to take revenge

Goals	first he wants to join the organization "Dred" because he wants to take revenge for his dead brother; he wants to be together with Zoe and therefore risks a lot by trying to meet her and later hiding her; he distances himself from the goals of Dred and does not want to support them any more; he wants to flee with Zoe to the place that Grandma pointed out to her where they can be safe; he wants to overcome the restrictions imposed on him by society
Political views	first he is ruled by his personal hatred for all Subbies and wants to take revenge, thereby aggravating the tension between the two classes; later he refrains from believing in and using violence; he has a defiant attitude towards authorities: he falls in love with a girl who is considered unsuitable for him, but sticks to her; he risks dangerous consequences when hiding Zoe in the attic of his school and behaves in a poised manner when the police come searching for Zoe, and lies to them
Personality traits	violent; aggressive (kills Pete); courageous; resistant; calm and with consideration in a situation of crisis (confronted by the police searching for Zoe); assertive about his decisions (confronting Mr James with his FAIR-membership); clever; ashamed of his surroundings; caring towards his mother and Zoe
Role in the novel	male protagonist; presents the situation in a dystopian society through his eyes

First name	Zoe May
Last name	Askew
Gender	female
City of residence	Silverdale
Age	14
Family background	lives in a pretty house with her parents who belong to the privileged part of the society Zoe lives in
Educational background	attends a school in her privileged suburb where she receives a good education
Outward appearance	good-looking girl who wears the typical teenager attire: jeans and a pullover, sweatshirt or jumper
Problems	she gets into trouble at school for having written an offensive remark on an assignment sheet; her parents then decide to move away from their neighbourhood; she falls in love with Daz who lives in the Chippy part of town; they cannot meet without danger; therefore, she decides to flee to that part of town by riding underneath a trash truck
Goals	she wants to be together with Daz and therefore flees to his part of town; she wants to flee with him to the place that Grandma pointed out to her where they can be safe; she wants to overcome the restrictions imposed on her by society

Political views	she has a defiant attitude towards authorities: she risks disagreable consequences when writing down an offensive remark; she falls in love with a boy who is considered unsuitable for her, but sticks to him; she does not comply with the rule of not being allowed to leave her Subby area; she lies to Pohlman, the policeman; she tricks the police who are out to catch her and flees with Daz to a place where she is not allowed to go
Personality traits	courageous; resistant; calm and prudent in a situation of crisis; assertive about her decisions; clever; willing to endure sacrifices and disadvantages
Role in the novel	female protagonist; presents the situation in a dystopian society through her eyes

First name	Grandma
Last name	
Gender	female
City of residence	Silverdale
Age	104
Family background	lives in an apartment in a senior citizens' block in a part of Silverdale; she is Zoe's mother's grandmother and Zoe goes to see her regularly; they are on a good standing
Educational background	seems to have had a good education and a lot of common sense because she has acted as a politically active member for a long time and can still listen to Zoe's worries and give her reasonable advice
Outward appearance	
Problems	she founded the FAIR unit in Silverdale and now leads it again after a long time; however, she cannot talk to Zoe about her involvement because it would be too dangerous; therefore, she feels very unhappy when she talks to Zoe
Goals	as she founded the FAIR unit she wants to change the structure of society and help to overcome the social faults and the degree of discrimination that is prevalent in the existing society; she wants to be an understanding and close companion to Zoe
Political views	she is a kind of revolutionary in society because she wants to overthrow the existing system; she believes in the principles of FAIR: a peaceful co-existence of the members of the two different classes achieved by more equality and a fair distribution of opportunities and goods
Personality traits	caring for Zoe; courageous; lucid; visionary; clever; prudent (not telling Zoe about her involvement)
Role in the novel	acting the part of an understanding and wise adult, functioning like an authority giving advice in difficult situations

Component 3: A glimpse of hope in the desert

Personal data	Outward	Feelings and attitudes	Grade of adaption	Dreams/hopes	Fears	Others' reactions
Daz Name: Darren Barraclough Age: 15 Lives in the city centre where the "Chippies" live	• he has wild, greasy-looking hair and often wears a beat-up leather jacket	• feels very worried after killing Pete (p. 112) • feels concerned and even ashamed because he realizes that Zoe is not happy (p. 123; p. 127) • behaves in a poised manner when the police come searching for Zoe (p. 135) • behaves protectively and caringly towards Zoe when faced with the Dred gang and finally makes her flee with him (p. 151; pp. 153f.)	• kills a guy called Pete because he hurt him badly; does not agree with the principles of "Dred" anymore (pp. 105f.)	• talks to his teacher, Mister James, to ask him if he can hide Zoe (pp. 127f.) • unconditionally supports the idea of being together with Zoe • after the flight he wants to get to a safe place with Zoe (p. 154)	• is afraid Zoe might be caught by the police or told on (p. 122) • hides Zoe in the basement because he is afraid that the police will find her (pp. 129ff.) • Mick of the Dred gang threatens to kill him because he suspects him of having killed Pete (p. 135f.) • is terrified that the guy he sold the gun to will identify him to Mick and Cal (p. 140) • observers two Dred members ready to kill him; decides to flee (p. 148)	• his mother is mad at him for taking away the tucker stamps (p. 112) • some Dred members want to take revenge on him for killing Mick (p. 148)
Zoe Name: Zoe May Askew Age: 14 Lives in the suburbs in Silverdale	• good-looking girl who wears the typical teenager attire: jeans and a pullover, sweatshirt or jumper	• feels disgusted and appalled when she finds the Chippy kids playing with a corpse (pp. 115f.) • feels discouraged by the way of life of the Barracloughs (p. 125) • starts crying when she realizes under which circumstances she is living and that she will have to hide again (p. 132) • when trapped in the basement facing Cal and Mick she behaves calmly and prudentially (p. 150 – p. 154)	• is assertive about her flight from the suburbs and wants to be with Daz • agrees to hide in the attic of the school to escape the police facing unfortunate living conditions and willing to endure sacrifices and severe disadvantages (pp. 132ff.; pp. 137ff.) • cleverly escapes the school building after the search unit has entered it (pp. 145ff.)	• she rides underneath a trash truck in order to get into the city centre to be together with Daz → courageous and resistant (p. 107 to p. 111) • after the flight she wants to head to the safe place Grandma pointed out to her (p. 155)	• she is terrified because of her plan and extremely afraid to be caught (p. 107– p. 111)	• her parents do not suspect her of escaping (pp. 107f.) • Mrs Barraclough is not very happy about the prospect of Zoe staying with them because she fears problems for themselves (pp. 120f.) • Mrs Barraclough reprimands her for not having brought proper clothes (p. 124)
Grandma Age: 104 Lives in the suburbs in Silverdale			• founded FAIR, ran it for a long time and now is active again; however, she never spoke to anybody about her involvement (pp. 142f.)			• Zoe admires her a lot for her involvement and considers her to be a close companion (p. 144)

Comprehension (pp. 105 – 112)

While reading pages 105 to 112, tick off the correct version of the following statements.

1. Daz kills Pete with his gun because

   ☐ a) Pete threatened him once.
   ☐ b) he cannot control his gun at this moment.
   ☐ c) Pete once knelt on his back while Mick rammed his face in the muck.

2. Zoe does not sleep all night because

   ☐ a) she is imagining several scenarios that can happen when she tries to take the trash truck outside.
   ☐ b) they are moving into another area.
   ☐ c) she had a fight with her parents the night before.

3. Zoe has the idea of taking the trash truck out

   ☐ a) because it is a common way of leaving the suburbs.
   ☐ b) after she read about this method in the papers.
   ☐ c) because it is the easiest way after bribing the truck staff.

4. At the gate the trash truck has to pass to get out

   ☐ a) the bouncer does not even leave his position.
   ☐ b) Zoe experiences a frightening moment in which she could be detected.
   ☐ c) the truck is carefully scrutinized.

5. Daz's mum is mad at Daz when she finds out that

   ☐ a) Daz has eaten all the food that was left.
   ☐ b) Daz has not given away the gun.
   ☐ c) Daz has taken all the tucker stamps.

Put yourself in the position of Daz's mum and write a diary entry about your life with him in the shabby apartment in the Chippies' ghetto. Write down your thoughts and worries about his absence during the previous night considering the fact that you already lost one son due to his involvement with Dred.

ns (pp. 113 – 122)

Find 10 words from p. 113 to p. 122 in this grid (↓ ↑ ↔ ↖ ↗ ↙ ↘).
Fill them into the sentences.

	A	B	C	D	E	F	G	H	I	J	K	L	M	N	O
1	m	a	h	k	l	i	p	l	m	n	b	g	f	s	n
2	l	o	k	b	v	s	c	r	w	d	n	c	u	o	n
3	q	w	u	e	e	v	m	b	n	m	s	l	i	x	d
4	t	s	r	n	e	w	q	o	v	q	l	t	i	i	u
5	y	u	x	m	d	c	c	v	u	b	a	n	m	m	w
6	e	s	w	u	a	m	l	e	p	l	o	i	o	h	m
7	y	p	x	d	c	c	a	g	o	h	d	h	e	j	k
8	w	i	e	d	r	l	t	s	y	z	u	e	i	o	p
9	a	c	s	y	i	d	e	f	x	f	z	g	r	g	h
10	a	i	y	n	x	d	c	v	a	i	v	b	n	e	m
11	w	o	g	e	r	t	t	z	l	u	i	o	p	p	d
12	k	u	j	h	g	f	d	y	a	f	g	h	j	k	l
13	y	s	x	c	v	b	n	m	g	m	n	b	v	g	h
14	r	w	e	r	t	z	c	o	r	p	s	e	u	i	k
15	z	u	i	o	p	g	n	i	n	n	i	r	g	c	d

1. The forest _____ for days after the terrible fire.
2. A _____ consists of millions of stars.
3. The assistant looked at the _____ of papers on the desk.
4. The family was left in _____ after the earthquake in which their home was destroyed.
5. This story sounds somewhat _____ to me.
6. The road into the forest looked extremely _____.
7. This woman is always _____ at me as if she does not take me seriously!
8. When the children saw the _____, they were terrified.
9. The animals were _____ out of panic.
10. The person spoke _____ as if she was inflicted by some kind of breathlessness.

Dystopias: Definition and characteristics

Utopia: A place, state, or condition that is ideally perfect in respect of politics, laws, customs, and conditions.

Dystopia: A futuristic, imagined universe in which oppressive societal control and the illusion of a perfect society are maintained through corporate, bureaucratic, technological, moral, or totalitarian control. Dystopias, through an exaggerated worst-case scenario, voice a criticism about a current trend, societal norm, or political system.

Characteristics of a dystopian society

- Propaganda is used to control the citizens of a society.
- Information, independent thought, and freedom are restricted.
- A figurehead or concept is worshipped by the citizens of the society.
- Citizens are perceived to be under constant surveillance.
- Citizens have a fear of the outside world.
- Citizens live in a dehumanized state.
- The natural world is banished and distrusted.
- Citizens conform to uniform expectations. Individuality and dissent are suppressed.
- The society is an illusion of a perfect utopian world.

Types of dystopian controls

Most dystopian works present a world in which oppressive societal control and the illusion of a perfect society are maintained through one or more of the following types of controls:

- Corporate control: one or more large corporations control society through products, advertising, and/or the media. Examples include *Minority Report* and *Running Man*.
- Bureaucratic control: society is controlled by a mindless bureaucracy through a tangle of red tape, relentless regulations, and incompetent government officials. Examples of films include *Brazil*.
- Technological control: society is controlled by technology – through computers, robots, and/or scientific means. Examples include *The Matrix, The Terminator,* and *I, Robot*.
- Philosophical/religious control: society is controlled by philosophical or religious ideology often enforced through a dictatorship or theocratic government.

The dystopian protagonist

- often feels trapped and is struggling to escape.
- questions the existing social and political systems.
- believes or feels that something is terribly wrong with the society in which he or she lives.
- helps the audience recognize the negative aspects of the dystopian world through his or her perspective.

While-reading assignments (pp. 123 – 134)

Answer the following questions.

1. Why does Daz feel so bad after Zoe has moved in with them?

2. Why does Daz's mother not react enthusiastically when she sees what Zoe has brought?

3. What are the peculiar circumstances about washing the dishes?

4. What does the noise of the helicopter signify?

5. What is the worst feeling for Daz?

6. State the reason why Daz talks to his teacher Mister James.

7. Why do the cops not find Zoe in her hiding place?

8. State some reasons why Zoe feels so bad.

9. Why does Mrs Barraclough advise Zoe to put on old clothes?

10. Which favour does Zoe ask of Mister James and how does he react?

While-reading assignments (pp. 135 – 155)

In the given grid, there are a number of quotations taken from p. 135 to p. 155. Write down the deeper meaning behind them.

Quotation	Interpretation
1. You can see by his face he finks he got his dirty little pause on the peanuts alreddy. (p. 135, ll. 5 ff.)	
2. I got that rest, because it was going to be a busy day. To say the least. (p. 139, ll. 21 f.)	
3. Yea, well – they luck lyke thay mean biznis, know wot I mean? (p. 140, l. 12)	
4. Now Wentworth's out and she's back up the sharp end at the age of one hundred and four. (p. 142, l. 28 to p. 143, l. 1.)	
5. Daz, supported by Mick and Smithy, was still on his feet. (p. 153, ll. 5 f.)	

How to write a newspaper article

A newspaper article or report informs the reader about what happened somewhere. It provides answers to the five "Ws" and an "H" ("Who did what, when, where, why and how?"). Reports have to be objective, but there is a variety of articles that only want to entertain the reader.

Step 1

- Decide whether you are going to write an article to inform or to entertain the reader and think about how you can make it either objective or entertaining and sensational.
- Write down notes about the "who", "what", "when", "where", and, if possible, the "why" and "how" of the event. Decide on the sequence of the different points (e.g. to create suspense).

Step 2

- Begin your article with an introduction to the event.
- Use your notes while writing the article.
- Divide your article into paragraphs.
- Include adjectives, adverbs, etc. to create a vivid impression and, if possible, quote what other people said about the event.
- Write a catchy headline when you have finished.

Step 3

- Does your article contain enough detailed information or can you add some more?
- Is the article interesting and easy to understand?
- Is the headline attractive?
- How have you connected your ideas and sentences?

Characterization grid: _____

Personal data	Outward appearance	Feelings and attitudes	Grade of adaption	Dreams/hopes	Fears	Others' reactions

Component 4
What's left to say

In dem folgenden *Component* werden verschiedene Aufgaben vorgestellt, die als Abschluss zur Lektüre mit dem Kurs behandelt werden können. Man kann die Aufgaben in einer Lerntheke den Schülerinnen und Schülern anbieten oder einen Lernzirkel aufbauen. Es ist natürlich auch möglich, einzelne Aufgaben oder Texte auszuwählen und zu besprechen.

Zunächst kann man den Inhalt des Romans mithilfe der "*touch, turn, talk*"-Übung auf **Copy 27** rekapitulieren. Die drei Seiten von **Copy 27** werden kopiert und die Kästchen ausgeschnitten. Dann werden die Schüler und Schülerinnen aufgefordert, einzeln nach vorne zu kommen, ein Kärtchen zu nehmen, sich zur Klasse zu wenden und aus dem Stegreif zu ihrem Stichwort ein paar Sätze zu sagen. Erfahrungsgemäß macht diese Übung den Kursteilnehmern Spaß und regt zu vielfältigen mündlichen Äußerungen an.

Auf **Copy 28** findet man Blogeinträge von britischen Teenagern, die *Daz 4 Zoe* in der Schule gelesen haben und ihre Meinung zu dem Buch kundtun. Es bietet sich hier an, die Schülerinnen und Schüler dazu aufzufordern, selbst einen solchen Blogeintrag mit ihrer Einschätzung des Romans zu verfassen.

> **Lösungsvorschlag für *Copy 28*:**
>
> 1. criticism
>   - unbelievable story – young people cannot deal with such a dangerous situation
>   - "love" between Zoe and Daz is rushed and superficial and does not seem plausible
>   - too circumstantial
>
>   praise
>   - two narrators
>   - detailed description of characters
>   - Zoe is a relatable character
>   - one needs to get used to Daz's spelling, but then it is great
>
> 2. Individual answers – however, students should either support the criticism or give praise. The criticism or praise should be based on evidence from the text.

Copy 29 bietet eine Übung zum Thema Mediation. Der Auszug aus einem Artikel der Süddeutschen Zeitung (Abgeschlossene Luxus-Wohnsiedlungen – Reiche hinter Gittern) vom 22.11.2011 beschreibt eine Entwicklung, wie man sie aus den USA schon seit Langem kennt: Leben in *gated communities*. Die Schülerinnen und Schüler sollen basierend auf den Informationen, die sie dem deutschen Text entnehmen, eine Verkaufsrede auf Englisch für eine solche Immobilie schreiben und im Plenum halten.

> **Lösungsvorschlag zu *Copy 29*:**
>
> 1. - you need not water your flowers yourself
>   - a gate protects you from strangers
>   - you can only enter the premises when you know someone

- you feel safer
- you can show that you are rich

2. Individual answers – however, students should point out that there is a need for security and safety and that gated communities grant you that. You live in complete comfort knowing that no unwanted strangers will roam the neighbourhood.

Copy 30 stellt einen Song des jamaikanischen Reggae Musikers Bob Marley (1945-1980) und seiner Band *The Wailers* vor. *War* wurde zwar schon 1976 veröffentlicht und klagt die soziale Ungerechtigkeit an, von der afrikanische Staaten betroffen sind. Dennoch lässt sich ein Bezug zu *Daz 4 Zoe* leicht herstellen, da auch das System einer Klassengesellschaft zur Sprache kommt, das die unterprivilegierten Bürger sogar der elementarsten Menschenrechte beraubt. *War* war fester Bestandteil auf Bob Marleys Konzerten und Tourneen von 1976 bis 1980 und zählt zu den bekanntesten seiner Songs. Er basiert auf einer Rede, die Äthiopiens letzter Kaiser Haile Selassee I. (1892 – 1975) 1963 in New York vor den Vereinten Nationen hielt. Hauptthema dieser Rede war der Friede auf dem afrikanischen Kontinent.

Lösungsvorschlag zu *Copy 30*:

1. In his song *War* (published in 1976) Bob Marley demands equality for all races, social justice and human rights for everybody as well as political freedom for all countries, especially on the African continent. He warns the world that the Africans will not stop fighting for their rights until they will have reached these goals.

2.

device	function
antithesis	
l. 2	• to make the listener aware of racist ideas
ll. 5 f.	• to emphasize the stark contrast between different social classes
l. 31	• to point out the rightness of ending the injustice
anaphora (ll. 1, 5, 10, 13, 19)	to reveal the extent of the injustice
repetition of the word "war"	to stress the urgency of a change
future tense	to express the determination of the Africans to fight

3. The song's message is a warning to the world that the Africans will no longer peacefully endure racism, inequality and the denial of even basic human rights. They demand a moral and just situation for their nations and are ready to fight for this change.

The song talks about the unacceptable living conditions of many black Africans. Thus, the basic idea can be compared to the social and political situation described in the novel *Daz 4 Zoe*. The society of the novel is divided into rich and poor, Subbies and Chippies, "first class and second class citizens", as the song says. (ll. 5 f.). The citizens are not segregated by race, but by social class. The situation of many citizens of African states who cannot claim basic human rights (ll. 10f. of the song) such as the right to work, to vote, to health care, to education and safety from violence, can be compared to the situation of the Chippies in the novel who have to live in subhuman conditions without work, in unhealthy houses, with access only to a very poor education and in an environment full of violence. As the reader learns from Miss Moncrieff's history class, the Subby politicians even tried to deny the Chippies their right to vote (p. 41).

Touch, turn, talk

Daz	Zoe	Mr Askew
freeway	Del	Tabitha
Mrs Barraclough	Chippy	Subby
Silverdale	Rawhampton	chippying
Falkland Islands	Veeza-Teeza	*The Blue Moon*
lobotomiser	to be in a fix	Chippy grad you ayshon
brainwashing	the plan	to mope

Miss Moncrieff	surveillance	Galileo
twine	Minotaur	skeleton
Chippy lover	tunnel	Grandma
miracle	fences	Dred
trash truck	rifle shots	Cal
goodbye	Paul Wentworth	Lieutenant Pohlman
She give me el.	imitation of the Chippy's dejected gait	'Hey missus, come see what we got.'

panorama of desolation	I had no idea how bad it would actually be.	Get her out of here, son. Get rid of her.
dulleye	As the fan's engine faded I heard a siren not far off.	Wots the rottenest feeling?
FAIR	the space under the furnace	Mister James
hiding in the roofspace in the school	peanuts	Grandma as a member of FAIR
sheets of paper on the ground with 'Have you seen this girl?'	Cal and Mick waiting for Daz in his apartment	the shot and the agonized scream which follows it
the flight into the darkness	what they see on Pikney Hill	Peacehaven

Blog

Submitted by Anonymous (Oct 23, 2009)

When I read this book at the beginning I first thought it was going to be boring but what made it so interesting was the fact that there was two narrators so you can get a point of view from both characters. As I read more it got more interesting and it started to show what the point of the story is, and I also like the way Robert Swindell shows what sort of person the character is by having detailed descriptions of them and by the way they write. It really helped me to acknowledge them. So if you are going to read this book I am advising you to start now before you tempt yourself. Enjoy!!!

http://www.sffworld.com/brev/bi4629p2.html [19.12.2012]

Submitted by Khoa (Dec 14, 2005)

This book is based on a love story. It is about forbidden love between Daz and Zoe. They both live in two different environments. Daz lives in poverty while Zoe has the luxury of dwellings and a proper education. The whole world is against their love for each other, even their own families. They are on the run from the authorities, trying to stay together.

I did not enjoy this book at all. I find it hard to believe that they're about fifteen years old and they manage to do so much against the authorities.

http://www.sffworld.com/brev/bi4629p2.html [19.12.2012]

Madge Undersee's review (Dec 25, 2011)

I absolutely adored this book. My teacher lent me it to read over the holidays and it's just brilliant. I'd love to study it in school but apparently it's not on the curriculum anymore. Zoe is an extremely relatable character for me, I loved her from the second I was introduced to her. I was undecided about Daz's horrible spelling and grammar at first, but it grew on me and I loved it in the end. I read this all in about three hours, I need to thank my English teacher when I go back to school.

http://www.goodreads.com/review/show/250926787 [19.12.2012]

Catherine's review (Oct 25, 2011)

Separated by a high wire fence, Subbies and Chippies live in completely different worlds. The Subbies are surrounded by nice houses, nice schools, nice people and covered in a thick protected blanket where nothing could go wrong. Chippies live in mayhem, in poverty, grime and dirt, scraping by to make a living and forced to survive horrible conditions. But one night when a Subby girl (Zoe) ventures past the fence, to the clubs the Chippies are so famous for, she spots a boy (Daz) and falls in love at first sight. But he is a Chippy. So they can't see each other, and they sneak around and blah blah blah etc.

It is a really interesting concept, that someday in the future, those who are less in society will be cut from those deemed higher. But the 'love' between Daz and Zoe is rushed and superficial and does not seem all that plausible. There is no intrigue and continued flirty eyes. Just rush straight in there. Even the whole sneaking around doesn't help. Everything is a bit too circumstantial for my liking.

http://www.goodreads.com/review/show/224321103 [19.12.2012]

---

1. Make a list of criticism of and praise for Daz 4 Zoe that you can find in these blog entries.
2. Write an entry of your own stating your opinion of the book.

Abgeschlossene Luxus-Wohnsiedlungen
Reiche hinter Gittern

22.11.2011, 15:03
Von Melanie Staudinger

Wenn Wohlhabende sich abschotten: Die Häuser stehen akkurat nebeneinander, die Blumen gießt der Concierge – und ein abgeschlossenes Tor schützt vor Fremden. Hermetisch abgeschlossene Viertel, soge-
5 nannte Gated Communities, gibt es nicht nur in China, Russland und Ägypten. Sondern auch in München.

Die weißen Häuser am Ende der Winzererstraße sind unübersehbar. Sie sind nicht nur neuer als die an-
10 deren Gebäude, die eher an Plattenbauten im Osten erinnern. Sie stehen auch alleine am Ende der Straße, direkt neben dem Olympiapark und einer Kleingartensiedlung. Richtig gefährlich sieht es hier in der Gegend nicht aus.
15 Und doch sind diese weißen Häuser, in deren Mitte zwei Brunnen einen großzügigen Platz schmücken, eingezäunt. Auf einer Seite werden sie sogar von einer knapp zweieinhalb Meter hohen Mauer geschützt, die nur unterbrochen ist für die Feuerwehrzufahrt.
20 Tilman Harlander kennt sich mit abgeschirmten Siedlungen aus. „Da kommen Sie nicht rein", sagt der emeritierte Professor für Architektur und Stadtplanung an der Universität Stuttgart.

Damit hat er recht. Durch das Tor am Eingang gelangt nur, wer drinnen jemanden kennt. An diesem 25 Vormittag ist nicht viel los. Aus der Wohnanlage hetzt eine Frau mit Kinderwagen. Zeit für ein Gespräch hat sie nicht. Über die Gründe, warum sie lieber von der Umwelt abgeschottet lebt, will sie erst recht nicht reden. 30

Richtig hermetisch abgeschlossene Viertel, in der Fachsprache Gated Communitys genannt, gibt es in Deutschland kaum. Bekannt ist der Barbarossapark in Aachen. Schlagzeilen haben auch die abgeriegelten Wohnanlagen in Potsdam, Berlin, Münster und 25 Leipzig gemacht.

Harlander hat sich viele solcher Viertel angeschaut – in den USA, in Brasilien, Südafrika, Russland, Ägypten, China oder Polen. Alleine in Warschau seien seit der Wende gut 400 Gated Communitys 40 entstanden, sagt er. In seinen Studien hat er herausgefunden, dass Menschen dort entweder leben, weil sie sich sicherer fühlen, oder weil sie zeigen wollen, dass sie Geld haben, viel Geld.

„Reiche hinter Gittern", Melanie Staudinger, www.sueddeutsche.de [22.11.2011]

---

1. Read the text carefully and take notes about advantages people see in living in gated communities.

2. Imagine you are a real estate broker. Write a speech informing a group of interested buyers of the advantages of buying a property in your gated community. You may use additional information from the internet:

    - http://www.realestateabc.com/insights/gated.htm [19.12.2012]
    - http://www.holidayhometimes.com/overview/buying-land-vs-buying-gated-community1962.html [19.12.2012]

Bob Marley and the Wailers: War

Until the philosophy which holds one race
Superior and another inferior
Is finally and permanently discredited and abandoned
Everywhere is war, me say war

5 That until there are no longer first class
And second class citizens of any nation
Until the colour of a man´s skin
Is of no more significance than the colour of his eyes   **significance** importance
Me say war

10 That until the basic human rights are equally
Guaranteed to all, without regard to race
There is war

That until that day
The dream of lasting peace, world citizenship
15 Rule of international morality
Will remain but a fleeting illusion   **fleeting** passing quickly
To be pursued, but never attained
Now everywhere is war, war

And until the ignoble and unhappy regimes
20 That hold our brothers in Angola, in Mozambique,   **Angola, Mozambique** African states that became independent from Portugal in 1975
In South Africa in sub-human bondage
Have been toppled, utterly destroyed   **to topple** to overthrow
Well, everywhere is war, me say war

War in the east, war in the west
25 War up north, war down south
War, war, rumours of war

And until that day, the African continent
Will not know peace, we Africans will fight
We find it necessary and we know we shall win
30 As we are confident in the victory

Of good over evil, good over evil.

War performed by Bob Marley and The Wailers
Words & Music by Carlton Barrett and Allen Cole
© Published by Blue Mountain Music Ltd.

---

1. Summarize the contents of the song in about 50 words.
2. Choose the three stylistic devices that you consider most remarkable and explain their function.
3. Point out the message of the song and comment on it in the context of the novel *Daz 4 Zoe*.

Bildnachweis

S. 3, 35: Victor Prischtt; **S. 6:** Picture-Alliance/Photoshot

Sollte trotz aller Bemühungen um korrekte Urheberangaben ein Irrtum unterlaufen sein, bitten wir darum, sich mit dem Verlag in Verbindung zu setzen, damit wir eventuell erforderliche Korrekturen vornehmen können.

EinFach Englisch
Unterrichtsmodelle

Herausgegeben von Hans Kröger in Zusammenarbeit mit Carmen Mendez

Ausgewählte Titel der Reihe:

Cultures in Conflict?
Literature on Ethnic Relationships
115 S., DIN A4, kart.   Best.-Nr. 041220
Audio-CD: 74 Min.   Best.-Nr. 062407
Textausgabe: 148 S.   Best.-Nr. 041218

**Echoes of the Empire.
The Mixed Voices of a Colonial Past**
20th Century English Short Stories
119 S., DIN A4, kart.   Best.-Nr. 041223
Audio-CD: 78 Min.   Best.-Nr. 062405
Textausgabe: 168 S.   Best.-Nr. 041224

Political Speeches
Historical & Topical Issues
127 S., DIN A4, kart.   Best.-Nr. 041236
Audio-CD: 70 Min.   Best.-Nr. 062409
Textausgabe: 132 S.   Best.-Nr. 041234

Utopia and Dystopia
Exploring Alternative Worlds
92 S., DIN A4, kart.   Best.-Nr. 041204
Textausgabe: 92 S.   Best.-Nr. 041202

Bend it Like Beckham
Filmanalyse
86 S., DIN A4, geh.   Best.-Nr. 041212

Dead Poets Society
Filmanalyse
67 S., DIN A4, geh.   Best.-Nr. 041255

East is East
Filmanalyse
101 S., DIN A4, kart.   Best.-Nr. 041228

Four Weddings and a Funeral
Filmanalyse
115 S., DIN A4, kart.   Best.-Nr. 041178

An Inconvenient Truth
Filmanalyse
91 S., DIN A4, kart.   Best.-Nr. 041186

Outsourced
Filmanalyse
110 S., DIN A4, kart.   Best.-Nr. 041172

Slumdog Millionaire
Filmanalyse
90 S., DIN A4, kart.   Best.-Nr. 041189

Don DeLillo: Falling Man
99 S., DIN A4, kart.   Best.-Nr. 041181

**Mark Haddon: The Curious Incident
of the Dog in the Night-Time**
99 S., DIN A4, kart.   Best.-Nr. 041252

**Mohsin Hamid: The Reluctant
Fundamentalist**
92 S., DIN A4, kart.   Best.-Nr. 041171

Lorraine Hansberry: A Raisin in the Sun
98 S., DIN A4, kart.   Best.-Nr. 041241

Nick Hornby: About a Boy
inkl. Filmanalyse
93 S., DIN A4, kart.   Best.-Nr. 041245

Nick Hornby: Slam
123 S., DIN A4, kart.   Best.-Nr. 041248

Aldous Huxley: Brave New World
93 S., DIN A4, kart.   Best.-Nr. 041249

Hanif Kureishi: The Black Album
114 S., DIN A4, kart.   Best.-Nr. 041179

Nick McDonell: Twelve
100 S., DIN A4, kart.   Best.-Nr. 041194

Robert Swindells: Daz 4 Zoe
91 S., DIN A4, kart.   Best.-Nr. 041170

**Tennessee Williams: A Streetcar
Named Desire**
102 S., DIN A4, kart.   Best.-Nr. 041238

Schöningh Verlag
Postfach 2540
33055 Paderborn

Schöningh

Fordern Sie unseren Prospekt zur kompletten Reihe an:
Informationen 0800 / 18 18 787 (freecall)
info@schoeningh-schulbuch.de / www.schoeningh-schulbuch.de